The Cure for Sleep

The Cure for Sleep

MEMOIR OF A LATE-WAKING LIFE

Tanya Shadrick

WEIDENFELD & NICOLSON

First published in Great Britain in 2022 by Weidenfeld & Nicolson,
an imprint of The Orion Publishing Group Ltd
Carmelite House, 50 Victoria Embankment
London EC4Y 0DZ

An Hachette UK Company

1 3 5 7 9 10 8 6 4 2

A CIP catalogue record for this book is available
from the British Library.

ISBN (Hardback) 978 1 4746 1807 6
ISBN (Export Trade Paperback) 978 1 4746 1808 3
ISBN (eBook) 978 1 4746 1810 6
ISBN (Audio) 978 1 4746 1811 3

Typeset by Goldust Design
Printed in Great Britain by Clays Ltd, Elcograf S.p.A.

www.weidenfeldandnicolson.co.uk
www.orionbooks.co.uk

For Eleanor and her daughter

The Female equally with the Male I sing.
Of Life immense in passion, pulse and power

Walt Whitman, *Leaves of Grass*

Author's Note

IN A FEW CASES, names and other identifying details have been omitted or changed, but there are no composite characters. I have tried throughout to protect the privacy of others, while retaining the right to tell and share my story. The many strangely timed events in the book happened as and when I say they did, and despite my resistance to ideas of fate or design.

All section epigraphs are from Walt Whitman, wisest and wildest of the poets I turned to in my second life.

Contents

The Light

DID I SEE IT?

What people want to know when they learn about my sudden near-death at thirty-three.

Yes, I saw a light, I say.

It changed me. But not in ways that were quick or comfortable.

I practised no faith before it, and none since.

And I can't know if what I glimpsed was the realm of God or physics, or just an effect of my body draining fast of blood and oxygen – only that it left me unable, on return, to sleepwalk through my days as I'd been doing.

I didn't rise from the hospital bed certain of purpose.

I hadn't been washed clean of my past.

I wasn't made saintly, or simply glad to be alive.

I was only more awake. A woman like stripped wire, pulsing with unstable energy, and seized by a need to escape my narrow self and circumstances, whatever the cost. But as a new mother in a small town, long married to a loving man?

There was more than myself at stake.

LAST MINUTES

a slipped skin

Space and time!

After Birth

IT WAS A CRISP WINTER AFTERNOON when the brisk midwife paid her last visit to the wren's nest of a house my husband and I had made for ourselves. We'd been proud to show her our few rooms, kept fresh as the outside day: our love of housekeeping being still more satisfying to us now our long-awaited child had come.

'Such a lovely home! And how well you've healed. What a neat mend!' she said from the step, going away.

I closed the door and really stretched for the first time in a fortnight: relieved, relaxed, cat-happy.

Our son, who'd set life ticking right again after three breath-held years of trying, tests and treatments, was sleeping steady in his basket. Like my grandmother's mantel clock years ago, the sound of him made me feel safe and secure – and this was the most I hoped for (or so I always told everyone) after my childhood in a fatherless and then frightening household.

Just feet away in the kitchen of our two-up two-down, my good husband had his back turned, making tea.

We'd met at university, aged just twenty, Nye and I: each of us privileged to be first in our families to study for a degree, while suffering (secretly, until we met each other) from a loss of belonging. Because that is what it required of us: that we *go away* for an education – the same phrase used by his people in Wales as mine in Devon.

Just one college in the whole country, near sea and built beside farmland on the Sussex Downs, felt possible for me who'd never been without fields and beaches. An instinct confirmed when its prospectus opened like a promise of good fortune onto a photo of Virginia Woolf. One of the few women writers I'd already read, I learned then that she had lived nearby, surrounded by like-minded thinkers. A way of life I wanted for my own, after being a misfit always, in school and out.

Yes. If she had chosen that landscape, it would do for me too. I assumed, straightforwardly, that if I only got myself to that more cultivated place and did there as she had, then in just a few years I'd grow into a life of use and beauty too. Maybe nothing so fine as an artist or writer, but part of something creative, instead of only working to earn a living as my relatives had.

But even that small campus with its few cafés and common rooms was several times the size of villages I'd known growing up. And to have so many people all around overwhelmed me, so that I stumbled homesick into the woods each day after class, cramping with culture shock. *Alder, birch. Charolais, Friesian. Hornbeam, knapweed.* I would walk and recite an alphabet of my known world to ward off panic got from seminars in the hard new languages of philosophy and art I'd been so impatient to learn.

What was I thinking, I said to the sheep one very bad day. *That I could uproot myself, when I come from stock that goes back so far, so deep, in one small place?* Like a horse refusing a fence, I began to spend most of my time alone. Sleeping outside during daytime instead of going to lectures. Declining invitations to go places, do things, until my fellow students stopped asking. Even going to the library for books made me run back, empty-handed. There were so many chances to connect and grow – clubs, societies, auditions – but it was too rich for my system. I shrank from it all.

Walking into a room at the end of my first year and finding Nye there rescued me from the challenges of social life. Within a month of meeting, we decided on a shared future: country girl and miner's son, joined at the hand and hip, with everything proceeding for years afterwards like clockwork. We graduated, got good jobs and saved one of our salaries each month until – by our mid-twenties – we already had enough for a railway cottage in the middle of a little street below a castle in an old county town just minutes from the university. Wherein we burrowed down and began living like the sweet and silly figures in the storybooks from which I'd first learned the world. *The shoemaker and his wife*, we called ourselves: married shorthand for a life of practical skill and homemaking we'd admired in the grandparents who'd help raise us.

We knew how strangely old-fashioned we looked to people going past our window in that town where every sold house was gutted fast and refitted by builders (neighbours stopped us in the street to tell us so): such a *young couple* to be spending season after season scraping wallpaper, sanding wood, building bookshelves and reading aloud to one another of an evening. But routines and economy pleased us, and with the friends and life's purpose we yearned for still unfound, we tried to be content. Bedding in, we spent carefully and kept company with dead and distant authors, while waiting for the decisive event that might flare up and illuminate our path. In the meantime, it was enough, yes, to be safe and secure.

In this way – living in stories, dreaming of a different time – we drifted through the doldrums of our twenties. With the arrival of a child, we would, we swore, be braver, more bold. Set sail at last on adult life.

An Awful Rowing

THERE WE WERE, THEN, AFTER IVF, its two-week wait, the shape-shifting of pregnancy, an emergency Caesarean. Normal, clumsy, slightly frightened novice parents of a newborn boy. Synchronising at last with what we believed other couples our age were doing.

So daftly happy we were in those very first days back home from hospital. Making proclamations about our son's character to anyone who came close even though he was such a primitive thing with only a few reflexes, and ink blots for eyes. Wetting his head with great, bubbling streams of sound, drunk with relief at feeling in the ordinary flow of time again after the suspended animation of infertility treatment. Magnums of language! Jeroboams! Celebrating him with improvised songs during each washing and dressing, and bestowing a new name every hour – *Mr Squawk, Little Man, Stretch Armstrong*. Pledging, as we tended him with unpractised hands, that we would be brilliant for him. Funny, surprising. Open-minded, risk-taking.

Yet at the same time be not overwhelmed but organised, capable. Make sense from the scattered data of his days, so he would soon go through the night and hardly ever need to cry. We began – Nye a systems analyst, me a project manager, and both of us children of trained mechanics – to keep a ridiculous, meticulous list of his breastfeeds, bowel movements and nap times: a logbook we'd consult at two and three and four in the morning. Trying, in less than a fortnight, and despite our promises, to bring this vivid new life into the fold of our orderly one.

Yes, there we were.

Our second Sunday as new parents. The green and brown dough of my belly sore all over again from the kneading our strong-fingered midwife had just given me, but otherwise? Sitting pretty. The laundry put away. Food in the fridge. A boy sleeping in a basket on the floor where – three years earlier – I'd knelt beside Nye pleading for *just a little more time* after he'd asked, in tears, that we try for a baby at last (a child only ever seeming to me a force destructive to love and work, as I – newborn and needy – had been the wedge that severed my mother from her job and then my father).

But this was not that.

All was quiet, all was bright!

Our carefully husbanded calm seemed to have absorbed our child's arrival – and my fears of motherhood – with hardly a ripple.

'See how we can already find a little time to read?' said Nye, still in the kitchen.

Smiling in agreement, I reached for a book from the shelf and it began.

The blood.

So much of it!

Like a cow passing water, I stood with my legs apart, stupid-looking, mouth open, while my dress and the carpet darkened.

Oh. I shouted, not understanding why my voice was so small. *Quick. Come. Get help.*

'Should I really?' Nye's face came close, but he was holding the phone away from me and my incontinent urge to use it. (Shyer than me even, he was so disliking of fuss and bother that he'd almost foregone his life's ambition of becoming a parent rather than trouble the NHS for fertility treatment.)

I spread my legs a little wider and we watched the colour puddle at my feet. He made the emergency call with frightened hands and a miraculous ambulance already nearby arrived in minutes. The crew ran in and strapped me to a trolley, tipping me feet above head, as if I were an egg timer they'd upended. Pushing me then, backwards and fast, through our narrow hallway into their van, whereupon they set the siren going and drove me away – without last words or touch – from home, husband, son.

My body was going to hospital. My self, however, set out in another direction.

Where was I? (In no pain, I had mind enough to talk to myself like this.) Upwards and tidal slow, I was floating on a blackness that had distance, volume. Words and phrases began happening.

Spacetime!

And here I was, going through the dark towards a distant, tiny whiteness that *contained an immensity*. It was – oh why was I so far away still? – it was an *inhabited light* in which every being that ever lived had slipped its skin, and divisions, and prejudice; a portal to good intent, where anything in this earthbound life not simply kind and courageous was burnt away on entry. I travelled faster, glad to go, unburdening myself of old hurts and longings as I went.

Only then, as I gathered momentum, did awareness of husband and baby begin – lately, faintly – to exert a backwards pull. How I hated it. And if they'd each been ropes around my feet, I'd have bent down and let them loose. Kept going. Instead, I accepted – with sadness and deep fatigue – that I must make every effort to return.

I'M NOT DEAD I'M NOT DEAD I'M NOT DEAD

I bellowed this, over and again, with increasing force (although only my lips moved, I learned later, from the woman holding my hand). And each time I shouted, I came only a little further back, and with the unsteady motion got on a river, as if my voice and words were oars. *The Awful Rowing Toward God*: book by a poet who'd tried to die several times before she did. Yes. This was that. Where she had gone, I was going. Heavy now with duty, I fought the pull, even as I hoped it would carry me away.

The pain began.

Not the body. This was anguish. Of mind, soul: acute, unsparing. Regret – sharp and precise as a knife slipped inside an oyster shell – broke me open, exposing something raw, ugly and absolutely true.

My cowardice.

How disgusting, to have my face brought so close to it, as if being forced to my knees with my neck held near a bowl of my own waste.

All the times and ways I'd turned away from risk and opportunity: moments not even Nye knew about, and absent from my life's written transcripts. Parties I hadn't gone to, job offers I didn't accept, because I was without the right clothes, or shoes, or accent. Skills I never learned because I was too shy, too proud, to join with a group of other beginners. The jealousy that squirted in my stomach whenever reading in the weekend papers about those who had *created* something, as if their achievements were stolen from the reserves set aside for my own unrealised future (that wish to be a writer which existed only as pages in private diaries). Bitterer still: the sight of women my age walking together, when I'd been without a best female friend a decade, longer; never envying them any babies or small children, only their adult companionship.

These and more. Deep shames, held in some appendix-end of self, all coming back up.

And what passed for my status in the world: how separate it seemed now, like the gall around a wasp larva or the casing of a caddis grub. My degree result – strangely stellar for a working-class girl who'd grown up with so few books – and the scholarship it won me for a master's. Rapid work promotions. Being asked back to my old school to give a speech. Even the amount I'd read, so that I recorded each title in a little ledger; miser hoarding coin. All this had mattered to me, very much, but felt now like a shell in which my real self lay formless, and recoiling from contact.

Coward.

Admit it, if only to myself, in whatever new dimension it was that had cast me into such hard light.

How little I'd given. Or gone for.

Living through the words of others, when I might have dared to share my own.

Hiding in an office. Even (yes) my marriage and reluctant pursuit of motherhood.

And now?

That crabbed life of mine was ending.

With dishonour on me, who'd wasted it.

A Matter of Life and Death

NOT THE AFTERLIFE, although it was staged that way: white-coated figures, haloed by light, weighing my fate on a scale.

Seven, eight hours I'd been there now, wherever it was the ambulance delivered me. Limbo, purgatory. The length of a whole working day in my life of the previous month! And there was a new routine as a mother to learn: the other women I'd only just met would be wondering where I was at our new group the next day – we hadn't exchanged phone numbers yet.

What was the formula for calculating blood loss from the weight of a bed sheet? A junior doctor to a young nurse, flirting together at the end of this bed I'd somehow arrived at. *He'd been working so long today already and just couldn't remember. Could she?*

The nurse laughed. A high, giddy sound that made me want to shake her, hard. Hysterical girl. Behave yourself.

Oh, she was rubbish at equations during training . . .

They smiled at each other from under their eyelashes. Intimate. Fond.

'How much blood have I lost, please?' I stared at them hard, unblinking, but they were blind to me.

'Oh, it's rare to haemorrhage as you have so long after delivery, but you'll be fine now. Women lose bottles of blood, a bucketload, with this. But you're all topped up with fluids.' Like a garage mechanic, the doctor didn't look at me as he spoke, all attention on the spring balance he was connecting, with the nurse's help, to a hammocky contraption. They began then, still billing and cooing, to bundle my bedding into it.

What sort of bottle, how big a bucket?

Before I could ask, their chatter at the end of the bed fell quiet. I watched them draw apart, exchange looks. Appalled. Silent. Frightened.

The sheet slapped the floor, heavy and wet, when they dropped it and ran from the room.

'I'm still dying,' I told Nye in this first minute alone together.

'You aren't, love. Don't worry. You can't be.'

I didn't persist. The air was shallow of a sudden, and hard to reach. Last bit of a fizzy drink sucked through a straw. *Save your breath*. How funny. All the adult catchphrases of childhood flooding back. *Don't come running to me if you fall and break your leg.*

Silent, painful laughter started to squeeze my chest, as when my boy cousins would pin me down with tickles till the thrill twisted into a fear of suffocation.

Cat got your tongue?

What did your last servant die of?

I was trickling.

The consultant had the dark-suited look of a stage magician. All these odd characters who were appearing as I shrank and faded: Wonderland, and I was Alice. My smile spread wider.

'That's good, yes?' said Nye. 'It sounds like a thing getting thin and stopping . . .'

No. It was very serious. Since my arrival, they'd been using a drip to constrict the vessels and slow things down – standard procedure – but instead it had been masking a much more dangerous arterial bleed. A minuscule amount of retained placenta had likely come away and torn an artery as it did.

Incredibly bad luck. And such massive blood loss meant there was now a real chance of cardiac collapse. An emergency operating theatre was being prepared, and he would do everything he could . . .

'But she is talking. Breastfeeding.' Nye gestured to me with our son in my arms, living proof.

Already at the door, going away, the consultant stopped and looked back.

'Your son is so new you probably haven't thought about what you'd do in the event . . .'

He paused to breathe deep, as though low on air himself.

'. . . so I will give you just a moment now before sending in the porters in case there is anything you want to say to one another.'

Husband and wife, side by side. The same shy and amateur-dramatic sensation felt on our long-ago wedding day, posing by the cake.

'Um. Does he mean how shall I feed Little Man while you're having the operation?'

'No, love. He means I might die. He means what will you do if I don't come back.'

'Oh. Well what, then?'

I closed my eyes and got an absurd, unbidden vision of Nye and a small boy spinning on hilltops. *The Sound of Music.*

'Take him home to Wales. Be there after school each day. And never tell him things don't hurt when he tells you that they do. *Promise.*'

He promised. We kissed. Then giggled. Tried next for more dignity, only to laugh out loud at finding our last words done too quickly with this awkward time left over.

The anaesthetist had the face of an angel. Faded gold hair, soft skin.

Unlike all the others before her, she bent very close and put her hands to my cheeks. She was so, so sorry. In the rush, I'd been brought to her on the wrong bed and so she couldn't put me to sleep here in the usual room. And I was so very ill that we might not be able to wait for one. So she would need me to be very brave and very calm and listen while she told me what to expect.

They were going to try very hard to save my life. Through the doors there was a large team, already robed and masked. Almost twenty people. And it was so cold in there, like a big walk-in meat freezer. Patients never felt that usually. I would be placed on the operating table, which was very hard and narrow, and so it was important that I didn't panic at that and fall. She would be there the whole time holding my hand and I would be fully under before the surgery began. *Did I understand?* So now she was going in to check they were ready and it was my job to find some way to quiet my mind and steady my breathing. *Could I do that?*

Alone then, grace came.

Not the raw animal struggle I feared would take hold and have me fight hands that might help, even while I begged for rescue.

Neither God the saviour, nor any of his host.

Nor was I enfolded in that alluring light I'd only glimpsed in the distance while being driven to hospital the day before.

What arrived was my own younger self: girl of nine who knew already she would have to work hard and keep herself safe.

She had come now, bearing courage. To remind me.

We had been doing this all our life: making meaning from what we could not escape or change. Living among adults who were angry, absent, depressed and disappointed: hadn't we wanted first to cure them, bring them back? Restore what they'd lost? Have them look up, out? And then, when we found that we could not, didn't we bend our vast and quiet concentration – inwards, outwards – on learning how to get away and reach firm ground? Only to find now, in this terminal moment, that it was not in a home or a job or even a savings account that we'd made this for ourselves. The stronghold was our *own mind*, filled with all the lives we'd ever admired and studied, so that we could *choose* – even until our last breath.

How to live. How to die. How to reach back with understanding, even as we are going beyond the ones we've loved.

In that perpetual minute which I believed might be my last, time past spread itself out like a quilt. I held my life to the light, studying its pattern and rips and repairs. Determined – if only for my own self-respect – to die wise, clear-sighted. The most awake I'd ever been.

FIRST LIFE

digger, dreamer

The girl and the wife rest the needle a moment
and forget where they are

WHERE DOES IT BEGIN, our turn away from risk and adventure? Why do so many of us hide in routine, shrink from opportunity?

What I asked in that luxurious last minute of living, my fear disappearing into wonder even as I was laid awake on the operating table.

Where does it begin? What I ask again, in this story of my life before then, and since.

For if the events which wake us are sudden, what leads to a sleep of soul and possibility is harder to trace.

We have to go back through all the tales told to us (or by us) about the world and its workings: that bramble thicket in which we lost our will and way.

Child

I wrap a body and lie in the coffin,
It is dark here underground . . . it is blank here, for reasons.

Bedtime Stories

I CAME TO CONSCIOUSNESS FIERCELY AWAKE. Destructively so, Mother told me – my refusal to go quiet at night (unless laid naked on her chest in the marriage bed) being a reason my father left us before my second birthday for a woman in the town below.

The me of three, of four, listened to her (as it was my role to do), and agreed. There was, until my birth, a husband and wife together for seven years, who were not now. They loved cars and built these rooms around me: the first words I ever read aloud and asked about were relics of that lost time.

Graemar? Burned into a little wooden sign by the front door we never used. Bits of my father's first name and hers, put together in the style of that time, Mother explained.

WE 2R1? Raised white letters on an oblong strip of black plastic in among the wedding photos. *Oh, that?* A joke, tied to the back of the car before they drove off on honeymoon – a fun number plate, saying the two of them were joined in marriage.

Now, could I leave Mummy be a minute?

Yes, there was something too-awake in me from the start that was not inside the few other small children I came close to – my same-age cousin, the girl down the lane. The ones at playschool: I took them into corners, behind curtains, to test them, like a doctor does. *Could they say the words I'd written? Did they know the proper names of what inside them made the thumps and rumbles?* I felt sorry for all they didn't know . . . but I envied them too.

From our storybooks, I knew myself the wolf or fox, and those other children around me the goats, the geese. Yet in the way of those tales, they had the better of me always and I'd have swapped places if I could. Their happy talent for napping on command late morning, so our minders didn't dislike them as they did me. How their mothers collected them after lunch, while only I and an orphaned boy being raised by his grandparents stayed till the end of day: an event which made me daily sick with sorrow, annoying the helpers even more. *Stubborn girl. Difficult child.*

Nursery hours were only ever this: an enervating lesson in difference so that illness became my favourite state – one I prayed for and practised with religious fervour, my body soon learning how to make the high temperature and sore tonsils that would gain me entry to the bliss of my Granny Shadrick's house while Mother worked. Only there – tucked in beside the fire she lit daily – was I ever left quiet to my own devices: maker of a wordless world on an old eiderdown quilt, queen over my cotton reel and clothespeg people.

Those, then, were my days. Exhausting, for the most part. And my nights? These were more strenuous still.

How it was to be Mother and me each evening, alone in that last detached bungalow of a tiny settlement on a lampless lane that faced onto an unheeding horizon of field after distant field: frigid, frightening. A state of constant alert that kept my small body taut as a tripwire.

Without a television, and only able to afford a little electricity, we scurried each dusk along the cold hallway before darkness came down. Bolting the hollow bedroom door behind us, Mother drank strong cough mixture to make her drowsy while I – aged three, four, five – kept guard, rigid and wakeful beside her. The black of country night pricked white in my eyes and noise from the fields pressing in on us had my blood thud with worry: the cough of a cow was always a man outside the thin windowpane; a fox making its rounds was a burglar trying latches. (Too scared to go beyond the bedroom at night, we took a bucket with us in case we needed to pee before morning.)

I had a way of playing with Mother's heavy black hair that soothed her, and this was my job: to take a small soft strand between my fingers and stroke it to a precise rhythm – picking it up, letting it fall – while she went on till sleep with the only tales it interested her to tell, and me to hear. A thousand and one stories of what there had been that was lost, which taught me the tangled roots of grown-ups, and mine in particular.

THE MAIDEN NAMES

Once upon a time there was my mother and her mother and hers before that. *Née, née, née.* Which meant their born name, got from the man that was their father whether he lived or died or stayed or went. But it was still something to know those girlhood names, before they married into another family, so I should learn them by heart.

Nor should I forget that whatever they had wanted was never, in the end, possible.

Little Granny – Mother's mother's mother – was happy to marry a poor local hedge-cutter, but hadn't expected marriage to make her the carer till death for her husband's three spinster sisters: one blind, one crooked and a beautiful third who had to be watched always so she wouldn't die for love of a married farmer (she slipped the latch one day and drowned herself; the ruby brooch in the jewellery box was hers, and would be mine one day because I resembled her so). When the last of these strange charges finally passed away – long after their brother, her husband – Little Granny was free to wish for what she wanted:

for Jesus to take her in the night so she could be with her youngest daughter who'd died at three of pneumonia. To this end, she put out her best burial clothes every night and hoped to be gone by the morning. (A small black-papered box was entrusted to us before she went: the relics of her little girl who lived for just a few years in the early 1900s – knitted mittens, a gone-brittle ribbon, horribly soft locks of butter-coloured hair kept wrapped in waxed paper. These, too, it was my duty to learn.)

Granny Nell – Mother's mother – wanted to be a nurse, but there was no money for training so she was a cook in the squire's house until an ill-matched marriage and six children. Her only ambition then was that her own offspring should never have to *dip their knee*, going instead into respectable work which kept their hands clean: the bank, the police force, the post office. Her children adored her as a mild-eyed martyr, but I resisted her dense gravitational field. I sensed, in a small animal's instinctive way, how her little sighs and wrung hands had made her family choose or stay in jobs that were against their nature. (She kept a jar of her gallstones on display and I understood, too, that this signified bitterness.)

LOVE AT FIRST SIGHT

The history of my mother's side was mournful, and set in a melancholic half-light of labourers' cottages tied to old estates, whereas the tales I begged her to tell me about my other granny's life seemed like one long summer, and became my paradise lost.

I loved best the story of Granny and Grandad Shadrick's courtship: a seven-year engagement during which they met once a week before evening milking and each Sunday after chapel in a few favourite gateways between his farm and hers. ('Why did they take so long?' I'd ask, knowing the answer but getting a shiver each time I heard it: that once a girl married away from one farm to another, she rarely left it afterwards – a wife always going back to visit her parents was judged harshly for *running the roads*. Good women were supposed to stay put, so that a move of just a half-mile up a lane upon marriage sealed off the path back to childhood.)

Love at first sight. How thrilling it was to my small, father-less self. The idea of being seen and chosen, at once, forever. I wanted it told to me over and over, with not a word out of place.

'That's the maid I'm going to marry,' tall and wavy-haired Donald said on walking into a social at the village hall one night.

'Well I don't have to say yes!' Dorothy said back, when he told her too. Squaring up to him, short as she was.

'Oh you can get a girl to do anything if you coax her right,' he said with a slow smile, and that – Mother said – was that. Years later, when she married their second son, my father, and moved onto the farm while the bungalow was being built, it was the older couple, Granny and Grandad, who were the lovebirds. Slipping off into the summer fields after tea and coming back late, hand in hand, covered in grass.

CAUSE AND EFFECT

But I was learning a darker story too. One in which even love could not protect against the accidents and emergencies that twisted lives out of shape – so that a small boy in the 1940s was already becoming the man who would leave his daughter. And where the threadbare life of Mother and me had been arrived at through a run of events that were as ugly and upsetting as dropped stitches in a piece of knitting.

If, if, if.

If Granny Shadrick hadn't been delivered of a stillborn baby – a longed-for girl – when my father was so small himself.

If she'd at least been given that lifeless child to hold, instead of it being carried from the room like rubbish.

If my father was more robust like his stout older brother

and not so nervous and needy that his stricken mother sent him away afterwards to her sister's.

If Granny hadn't, on his return, remained always somehow blind to him – the way birds can be to young that fall outside the nest – giving all her love and favour to the eldest boy.

If gentle Grandad Shadrick, who admired his younger son's mechanical skills, hadn't died without a will in the miss of a heartbeat so that Granny passed the farm to her older boy, telling my father he *had his hands* and could make his living in a garage.

If Father hadn't been wild with grief and injustice from all this when I was born just a year afterwards.

If my constant crying hadn't then reminded him of his own demanding self of long ago, so that what he disliked in himself he pushed away in me. ('Never ask me to hold her again,' he shouted at Mother in town the only time she put me in his arms a few minutes so she could fetch a prescription. So much raw and unappeasable need in my small body repulsive to him. Unforgiveable.)

If I'd been easier, prettier, with more winning ways.

Conclusion I came to. That child's instinct: to take the full weight of blame and shame rather than feel cast adrift in the universe by chance or carelessness or insignificance.

And that is what I suffered from most in those lightless nights of my earliest years: a wild shifting of size and shape, from being both burdened with worry and cut loose by Father.

While I listened to Mother's stories, stroking her hair all the while, my chest swelled with pride at our aloneness, making do without so many of the things nursery books listed as belonging to every home and family. During this part of bedtime, I guarded her with heart thumping hard, stiff and vigilant like a little tin soldier. It was a love to beat time and circumstance: *I would be her husband, or find her one, or make our fortune.*

But once she fell silent in sleep, I became prey to a flying-through-the-air sensation that came for me every night, in which my self was plucked from its body and carried high into the sky. A never-not terrifying ascent before the still worse that always followed after: my plummet back down so I became, over and again, a single strand of hair on my own head.

Oh how small I was, how powerless. Nothing much, and all she had.

Learning with Mother

HOW MUCH BOLDER WE WERE IN THE MORNINGS!

Up early so Mother could dust and hoover before long hours in the town's grocery shop, we'd breakfast in a rush (flimsy bits of diet bread for her, a sturdy boiled egg and soldiers for me) and turn then to the serious business of dressing for the day. Father's absence had left us exposed to pity and judgement, so we took elaborate care before leaving our fasthold on the hill: it was important to appear always neat, clean, attractive. We put aside our mournful habits upon waking – two thin nightgowns hung on a peg – and began spinning bright stories of our skills, our gifts, our value.

As in: *What black hair and blue eyes Mother had!* And by putting green shadow on her lids like this – *did I see?* – it brought out her unusual colouring even more. Other women might have more clothes and shoes, of course, but it was wasted on them because they didn't understand *elegance* like Mother did, and I was learning. Her only brooch, for example, a simple golden fern: almost every day someone complimented her on it, because she pinned it high, to the side, at an angle. And her beautiful dark eyebrows – which I'd been lucky to inherit – these must be plucked only from below the arch, never above, so as to keep their natural shape. *Was I watching?* Did I see, too, how by leaving just a few buttons undone at the front of her overalls it looked more like a dress, not a uniform? Perfume, remember, should only ever be used sparingly – *here on the wrists, then a dab behind the ears.*

There were rules like this for everything, mostly taken from *The Dairy Book of Home Management.* A wedding gift, this stern housekeeping guide was her constant reference and my first serious reading material: far more compelling to me than the silly little pastimes offered to children in my Ladybird *Learning with Mother* books. How strange, in those pages, to see grown women playing at zoos and tea parties all day when there was money to earn. More useful by far to sit at Mother's feet while she dressed, her housekeeping manual on my lap as I worked to understand the ways of the adult world.

THE ART OF MAKE-UP

This section (which Mother asked me to open each morning) was stuffed with instructions that confused further my already unstable sense of size and shape by advising that a woman could – in every instance – make more of herself through hiding, disguise, reduction. A big mouth required *unobtrusive colours kept well within the natural lines* and square faces could be moved towards the heart-shaped ideal by *sweeping crescents* of blusher. Feet were often neglected but *determined grace in walking, posture and even the expression on the face* so should be sanded hard with pumice stone.

As with the 'keep slim' exercises she also got from the book – rolling wildly side to side, pedalling her legs at the ceiling, flinging her arms outwards to lift her bust – Mother's fierce dedication to all these rituals alarmed and delighted me in equal measure. Looking at us both in the round mirror of her heady-smelling wardrobe, I was a frog next to the quick bright bird of her. Slow, dull-coloured, unlovely. I felt no envy, just admiration, believing I would never be likewise transformed. My only real unease came whenever she invited me to dress up myself – I became stiff then, and indignant, like a courtier who prefers a ritual distance from their mistress.

More content to serve – a pageboy not her daughter – I searched the carpet for lost earring backs. Cleaned out her handbag. Unzipped the knee-high leather boots for her to step into. *What a good girl I was.* To sit by her feet like this, helping her get ready for the tongues that wagged and the eyes that kept watch.

This was another early and disturbing glimpse of the system we existed in.

Because although it was Father who had an affair and left, it was Mother – the only single parent in our time and place – who paid the price. Back there, back then, a good reputation was one of the few assets a working-class person could accrue; conformity was the ruling principle, and anything which made you exceptional could cause your stock to fall fast in that small farming town with its weekly cattle sale at which people were discussed and evaluated just as much as land and livestock.

COST OF LIVING

While the tales Mother told at bedtime were all about love and loss, her morning stories were frank accounts of money and status: how to acquire and keep hold of them.

When she and her siblings first arrived in that market town from an outlying village in the 1950s, their father – somehow elevated by wartime connections from picking potatoes to manager of the new Milk Marketing Board – had impressed on them the same sort of lessons. Any chance of further advancement as a family could only be achieved by being respectable. No smoking, no drinking. (And if he ever caught them stood talking on street corners they would feel the back of his hand, old as they were.)

Funds were somehow found to send the eldest son away to grammar school, but my mother – next eldest and possessed of an equally quick intelligence – had to make do with the secondary modern. A rule-loving child, she took pride in her cheaper uniform and won prizes for maths, English and painting. And yet her favourite story was how the unmarried art master used to stand her on the table so everyone could look up and draw her *lovely figure*.

But even as she was enjoying this quite natural wish to be admired, her father had plans to hide her away: she would soon be sorting string in the back rooms of the town's hardware shop, and be engaged to the town's apprentice undertaker.

A daughter as an expense to discharge, a risk to be managed.

And so from the age of fifteen she began to bring home a weekly wage of one pound, a shilling and a few pence. Her father stood at the gate each evening to clip her round the ear if she was late back, and her mother took most of the money for lodgings: a strait-jacketed pattern of living so many girls of that class, that era, were confined to until released into the bonds of marriage. But there were a couple of pennies left over, and the freedom my mother squeezed from them had young me believe her the stuff of fairy tales, more than any serving girl whose life was transformed by wish or wand. She was my first exemplar of waking up: the time required, the effort.

NIGHT SCHOOL

For two years, twice a week, my mother in her late teens took evening classes in Pitman shorthand and typing. A strict, difficult training of many thousands of hours done around long days in the shop and helping at home, it made everything ache – arms, eyes, brain.

Why on earth was she wasting her time and her money? her parents asked, irritated by her ambition when she returned late, wrung out, to their overcrowded flat with mould on the walls and damp towels drying over the chair backs. Every week she would restate her stubborn hope to become a clerk in the National Provincial Bank, where her older brother was being trained as a manager, and they replied always with their own stock answer: *The banks only ever took on girls from grammar schools. It wasn't for the likes of her.*

By the time I was of age to be her audience, all that followed was already yet another story of paradise lost, but asking her about it was the surest way to lift her spirits and mine before we left the bungalow for the day. In its telling she slipped the skin of her tiring life – single mother with a long shift as a shop worker ahead – and was returned a while to her natural element.

'I just had the knack of it – *pee* was a light diagonal, *bee* was a heavy one – and so I soon had one over your grandad. He'd be going on at us and I'd take it all down, word for nasty word, and read it back to him before running away. Oh he used to dance with temper!'

I refused always her offer to teach me those simplest short-hand strokes, impatient for the part I never tired of hearing, or she of telling. Her time of *elevation*.

'Then one day when I was in the window of Whitlock's – laying out a dinner service display – there was a tap on the glass. And that was the dear old deputy manager of the bank, knocking with the pipe he used to smoke. They'd received excellent character references, he said, and I could join them from my next birthday. So the moment I turned nineteen I started, and although it was only just across the square, it was that saying, you know? *Going up in the world.* I went up in the world, I was walking on air, and I stayed that way the whole ten years I worked there. Every single day.'

THE JOY OF WORK

The bank! Oh, how she loved it! The status symbols: her name badge, the clerk's coat which *fitted like a glove*, the weekly pay packet which kept rising till it neared her father's. Rules and regulations that her orderly mind thrived on: single-entry ledgers demanding her best copperplate handwriting so whole afternoons passed in a happy bliss of bitten-lipped concentration; the end-of-day cash balance which had to be penny-precise before they were allowed home. Its feudal system of rank and etiquette relating to how each staff member and customer should be addressed.

There was, too, a performative element she lived for, that showcased her beauty even more effectively than the art master's table or the shop window. As cashier behind number one till at the National Provincial on market day, framed like a painting by its wooden booth, Maria Ann Stevens of the black hair and blue eyes was visited by every retired colonel and rich farmer in the surrounding area. A faster crowd came calling too: young architects, solicitors and surveyors with cars and qualifications.

This attention woke in her a new appetite for risk and adventure, where before she had been on a straight and narrow path to *better herself.* Now she began to sneak a life for herself in lunchtimes, driving down to the nearby coast with various admirers for just a few minutes in the water and the feeling it yielded for the rest of the afternoon – of being wildly alive under her neat outfits. Sexy after so many strait-laced years, to have sand and salt lingering on the skin.

She was still, at this time, engaged to the sweet apprentice undertaker while not understanding how advanced the plans for marriage were. Then a day came when the date was revealed; she fled from home in a breathless panic.

'I loved him dearly, and his parents, but I hadn't *lived*, was all I could think. It was as if my father was going to put me in a box and bury me. So that was it. I begged a widow for some lodgings that evening and left home. Twenty-two years old, and free at last.'

A NIGHT TO REMEMBER

Now it came to her, wave after wave, like the sea.

Status. Invitations. Would she go with this vet or that auctioneer to a dinner dance? Take the train up to London and stay in the Belgravia mansion of a young barrister who had holidayed in town with his parents for years, loving her from a distance? Become clerk to the area's newly formed Young Conservatives? Celebrate becoming a bright young thing by going with the group to skinny-dip under a full moon?

Every silver-edged detail of what she wore and cast off that one, unforgettable night was held up to my young, wide eyes; I learned them like the parts of a nursery rhyme: the height of the heels, the fit of the white wool dress she'd saved for and wore with a wide elasticated belt; the headscarf she tied under her chin in the style of Elizabeth Taylor to protect her hair in the fast, open-top car which carried her there; how the boy beside her kept stroking her arm and saying how *soft* she was.

But even as Mother reminisced, cavalier, about that naked moonlit swim, puritan-me peered into the shadows at the edge of her story. Began to reel her back from her happy trance with questions.

How had that dreamlike life led to her and me, alone in the bungalow? Why didn't she marry the barrister who asked her? When did Father, a mechanic interested in car engines and fishing instead of politics and moonlit swims, come along? Where did it go wrong?

'Well.' She'd pull a face. 'I tried to imagine the wedding of me and the boy from London. I wanted to join with him and his family, but I couldn't picture mine meeting his at the service. Father in a string vest with a fag hanging out his mouth. Mother in her cleaning overall. I was embarrassed, is the truth of it.'

And *my* father? Why him? How?

'I had a Morris Minor by then. One of the first young women in town to buy a car. I was *the envy*. This particular day it needed fixing, and I took it into the garage after coming back from a lunchtime dip in the sea, my costume drying in the back. Your father was the one who did the work. He said he saw my swimsuit and it gave him ideas. Leopardskin print, it was. My God I looked superb in it.'

It would be years still before I'd have a language for class, and longer again before I'd experience myself how it was to sleepwalk towards the familiar and away from the discomfort of opportunities I'd worked hard and long to open up. But I did from Mother's stories grow distrustful from a young age of anything too bright and too beautiful, which flew too high.

God the Father

BEARING WITNESS TO ALL MOTHER'S MEMORIES in my pre-school years left me with an unbearable longing to be seen and heard in turn. I placed a mirror on the floor each day and sang into it until my throat went croaky, imagining it a portal to both God and my father, the two men I yearned for. They lived together, I believed, in a realm I might reach only by song.

Our Father who art in heaven, hallowed be thy name. The Lord's Prayer, found in another of my nursery books: learned by heart as the only form of words I could find for what I lacked and wanted.

Give us this day our daily bread, and forgive us our trespasses. Singing to Father so many months without ever an answering sign that I began to forget my love had ever been anchored to a real man. It became instead a dream state, the heavy water in which I was suspended – longing without end, so that I began clinging to objects for more reliable contact. And the fact of his absence, which had come before I had words to show Mother how it hurt? This lived from now on as an ache in my stomach that refused any foods I had once shared with him. In these and other obscure ways, all my unhappiness either sublimated or suppressed.

What a terror, then, just as I was forgetting Father and looking forward to starting school, for him to be there of a sudden: in a part of the garden I never played in, and standing in the sun so his face was hidden and me cast into shadow.

And a nightmare in the waking day, to see my dearest possession being turned upside down in his hands like the engine pieces he took apart at work, his fingers stained black like the vice on his left-behind workbench. I was seized with unsayable discomfort. How could I, so small, find the words to make him stop what he was doing?

Because what a wonder it was to me, the Weather House. Barometer in the shape of an Alpine chalet from which a happy man and woman swung in and out.

I'd found it in a heap of things smashed in temper and forgotten in the rush back when he went away. Nothing had been left whole or working on that long-ago day, but each recovered treasure was infused now with the love I yearned to give and receive. Badger-hair shaving brush with cracked enamel handle; single, silver cufflink; bits of broken record from a kind-eyed country and western singer whose voice I longed to hear again: these and other cast-offs were my keepers of secrets.

As children who fear further loss often do, I kept these riches out of view: they lived in a box within a box at the far, muddy corner of my Wendy house where a grown-up would be unlikely to go. But I'd been ambushed that day, which is how it came to happen.

Quick, quick! Mother had said. My father was there on a rare visit. No, not inside the house, he wasn't allowed any more since *the divorce*. Outside in the garden. But he was only on a short lunch break so I must hurry. *Quick!*

I'd gone around the back of the bungalow, running my fingers along the pebbledash (another of my new, nervous habits: a compulsive touching so as to earth myself against the flying-in-the-air feeling got in the days now as well as the nights). My welly boots were slapping the backs of my bare legs and a new fear took hold: Father might be back to fetch his things, and shout at me for keeping them.

'Come give old Daddy a kiss.'

I sat beside him. Stiff. Shy.

'I've been missing your kissing, and nothing beats your loving.' Our first and only joke, gone a long time: words on the mug in which he used to have his tea on return from work each evening.

Silence between us. Loud with sounds of what I trusted. *Bees. Tractor. Cow. Donkey.*

'This is my new wife. Your stepmum.' He opened one of the pockets where my sweets used to be and brought out a photo. A woman with strange white hair was sitting in a field of poppies with her skirt spread out and a blouse slipped off at one shoulder.

'Pretty, isn't she?' I nodded, then shook myself inside. *Yes. No.* Confused by how much I understood always, but had no speech for. And the shifting of size and shape had begun again. How large I felt lying beside Mother through each vast night, a woman in waiting. Yet how small I was becoming here at Father's feet.

More questions then, too many, as adults use when nervous. *Did I want to ride on his back? Be swung around? Play penalties in between the fir trees like we used to do? With Daddy in goal, and I could have three misses?* I shook my head. How to say that the boys next door climbed the hedge and took my beloved orange ball for themselves? Throwing it back some while later, punctured, flat.

In this way, we arrived at my Weather House.

My favourite toy these days? What was it? Go fetch. I ran away, animal-glad to be released from the cold stone seat and dark bramble hedge behind it. My cautious habits cast aside.

There it was behind my rubble of egg boxes and other mud-pie making stuff. House within a house. Smelling of the soap scraps I'd collected from a wooden shaving bowl in among the heap of leavings. Pink smell of violets, now more dear to me than the man who had reappeared, bitter with smoke and engine oil. I rushed back and handed it to him.

'A toy, I said. Why bring this?' He frowned at it, but my words came pouring out, a snowmelt, now I'd been asked something I could answer. Because how I loved them, the little man and wife who were always there when I visited! What care I took collecting the best seeds and petals to push in through the lady's door so she could bake a cake! The amount of little twigs I snapped into tiny pieces so the man could keep the stove going!

I did not say it had been my whole body's wish – hands, heart, tummy – to make them come out at the same time, and how many hours I spent trying until I learned that they could not and would never. Nor did I tell him about lying stiff and wakeful beside Mother in the double bed at night, willing myself small enough to sleep inside the chalet with a bed of my own, able to wriggle when I needed, with the man there to check for noises when they came. None of this I spoke aloud, but what I had said was too much. Father's voice got loud.

'This isn't a toy.' He took out a small yellow-handled screwdriver from his overalls. 'It's a barometer.' I reached for it and was pushed away, my skin prickling like it did when Mother pulled a jumper full of sparks and static over my head.

'It's broken.' He put the screwdriver away and left the back of the chalet hanging off. I began to understand what would happen next, but was too short, too slow, to stop him.

Could only look, mute and useless, as he hurled the man, the wife and their house far into the thick, thorned hedge.

What happened after that?
White out.
Not the first time or last when memory got cut off in a storm of sorrow or longing. My feelings, likewise: whenever a situation threatened obliteration to my small self, a flare of blinding light happened in my head (the way camera flashbulbs went off back then). I rarely cried in those early years or had tantrums, so that

old ladies in town liked to stop Mother and praise me for being *a good little girl, coping so well.* Instead of any external signs of distress that might upset Mother in turn, only ever these short circuits and internal combustions.

And this is how it was that day.

Snap.

Anguish and its aftermath, gone.

As was Father when I came back to myself. Minutes later? Hours?

A mother and child alone again. She, back turned, pruning her beloved ornamental shrubs; me at the far edge of our large vegetable garden, with tearless eyes and lips set firm. My small stock of treasures laid out. Holes already dug.

Only the tiniest thing, the cufflink, I allowed myself to keep. The rest I buried, deep. Patting the soil over them like babies being put to bed. Imagining, as I did, that they might grow and then make more of themselves – while knowing they would not.

Weather House

IT CONTINUED LIKE THIS NOW. Father as a force of nature: an ill wind that blew in, whirling things away to the new family house he was furnishing in town.

We'd come home from our long days at work and nursery to find chairs gone, the table, tools from the garage – a blizzard of little losses, in which Mother and I (though umbilical-close still in bed) began to lose sight of each other. Both of us retreating into increasingly strange and separate ways to feel safe.

She began to rise earlier and earlier, exhausting herself – and me, hearing her – in a forensic daily dust and hoover of our every square inch. We'd always lived to a fixed routine, but the new household rules were stricter still. I left too many sticky marks (even though she had begun to wipe my face and hands between each bite of food) and so was not to touch, any more, objects from the mirror-backed china cabinet I'd press-ganged as companions: cheerful yellow coffee cups; willow-pattern serving plate that thrilled me with its story of two escaping lovers who turned into birds at the water's edge to escape their families. Nor could I push back our net curtains to look at the sparrows and cats that came to the window ledges: each fold was set in place by Mother's hand with the precision of a cake being iced.

Flour from baking, ash from the open fire in the best room, stains from paints: many of the things I loved produced residues that she now found overwhelming, and so the territory left for me to play in shrank daily. Even turning on the kitchen tap was forbidden: it ran too fast and splashed the tiles. Bowls of cereal, cups of tea: anything I wanted to eat or drink had now (and until I left home) to be asked for, and not attempted myself.

Having inherited my father's quick fingers – I'd already at four put together a simple lawnmower delivered in pieces that defeated Mother – I yearned for texture, tools. Impatient to master the world and its many moving parts, I was cut off from it first by loss of Father as guide, and now through my mother's fear of dirt and disorder.

Granny's house remained a small oasis where I was free to touch all my hands desired: buttons in a biscuit tin; slender-legged animals carved from dark wood I took down from shelves; playing cards I spread out and talked to as townsfolk. Balls of wool ripped back from old jumble-sale jumpers that I was allowed to weave between table legs, door handles and window latches, following the sunlight wherever it moved.

At home with Mother, I imagined myself to be separated by bramble and briar from things I loved and wanted, so I shouldn't reach for them and cause a mess or breakage. And began to transmute my need through reading, clinging to the *Book of Home Management* and all the less decorative sections my mother overlooked. PLUMBING. ELECTRICITY IN THE HOME. CARE OF THE CAR. MAKE DO & MEND. FIRST AID. It was an obsession with repair equal and opposite to Mother's worry of what might break or be taken away.

We were trying, in these ways, to control our environment, but the bungalow was as exposed to the elements as we to my father's visits.

We'd already survived the hottest year: time when the taps ran dry and we took buckets down the lane to a standpipe for our water. That long and infamous heatwave when our rooms – usually too cold – began to stifle us so that we lay at night under damp sheets, raw with heat rash, and panting, rabbit-breathed; too scared of intruders to open the windows (a house with stairs became after that my dearest wish).

And on one of those molten mornings, a new terror: we woke to the sound of hail and found the outside air thick with insects – a plague of ladybirds breaking shrubs with their weight and cracking nastily underfoot when we had to leave the house.

In the next year it happened with snakes: adders whose bellies spilled disgusting, pulsing eggs when one of us could bear to bring the hoe down hard enough. After that, butterflies that crumbled into dust as more and more of them landed on the buddleia bushes, each other, their pigment staining our garden paths, so that my growing worry at what was too bright and fragile in my mother spilled over into phobia. Moths, birds, the colour plates in our nature book – anything vivid turned my stomach. I began to live in black and white, confining myself to words and lines on paper.

Then, when I was five, the world went white too.

Mother pulled the bedroom curtains back one winter morning on a strange half-light and silence pressed like a padded mattress against the house. We stared a while, shivering, then flew frantic, caged, from room to room, trying every casement latch and handle.

All our windows and both doors: sealed shut by snow.

We ran next to the taps and switches.

No power.

No water in the kitchen.

No phone to call for help.

No television, no radio, to tell us how deep the snow, how widespread, how long it was likely to last.

What did we have?

Water in the bathroom. Heat from the oil-fuelled Rayburn. Candles. Matches. Beyond our usual small stock of fish paste, eggs and diet bread: a few tins of soup, a bag of sultanas. Each other.

Enough.

But it wasn't, of course. While we protected each other from panic with our usual exclamations of good fortune – *How lovely to make a nest by the stove! Wasn't the candlelight pretty!* – we had reached the limits of our insistent self-sufficiency, and knew it.

None of the men in our family came for us: not Father, or Grandad, or any of my uncles. And when we were dug out – days later, reduced to using stock cubes as broth – there were no handsome firemen or farmers at the threshold. We'd been saved by an old man, bent-backed, and his tiny, lopsided wife – an ancient pair, smelling of mothballs, from whom I always hid, breath held, whenever they called to collect our insurance stamps.

Who was worse off than them? They wondered to each other, once they were themselves squeezed free.

Mother, me.

Years later, a new undergraduate at my set texts, I would read about the last days of a poet, alone with her babies in a winter still worse than ours. Abandoned by her husband, reliant on the kindness of strangers. Bone-thin from flu. Tired, frightened. Humiliated. A lifelong effort to distinguish herself ending beside the gas oven of a frozen London flat. How many women, I learned afterwards, ended their own lives and their children's due to the stigma and financial hardships that came from being a single parent in those post-war decades.

My fingers throbbed against the page, eyes stinging with a sinus burn of held-in sorrow. I wanted to run to the communal phone I never used and talk to Mother. To ask, to hear, how it had been in those comfortless rooms of our long confinement – for her, not me. Really. To thank her for staying as my father had not.

I didn't call. It was too soon in my own break for freedom; I was brittle, resistant. Coldly determined that my life be different.

Young Woman

Think of loving and being loved;
I swear to you, whoever you are, you can interfuse
yourself with such things that everybody that sees you shall
look longingly upon you.

Survival Mode

TANYA FELL AND WENT TO SLEEP. All the girl down the lane will say, and keep saying, when she is discovered on the back step of the bungalow, crying.

The laundry drops away. Time and mind. The world. There is only this mother with a child – *dead? dying?* – in her arms. Blood is coming from her daughter's ears, nose, mouth, and the woman's throat soon tastes of iron after shouting itself raw for help that doesn't come from any of the fields or farmhouses. She stumbles to the lane's end where a slightly larger one bends down towards the town, and lays her – *gone? going?* – girl on the roadside. Where she stands then like every mother who has ever suffered the breaking of a child, her own body becoming prayer and plea. Beacon, distress signal.

A car goes past and does not stop. Another, another, even when she risks injury herself by stepping into their path. They go around, and down. And this destroys the last of what has held fast in her since the divorce: that refusal of others to see or stop.

§

The fall.

I did it to myself, on purpose, just minutes after our return from an unhappy holiday with one of the men who'd begun to circle Mother since I'd started school. Many of them (the married ones and fussy mothers' boys grown old) we only laughed about, whenever we came home to find perfume, fruit and flowers laid at our door.

Silly fools! We needed winter coats, fuel for the Rayburn!

But a few she let in, and this one, I knew, would ruin us.

Seized with presentiment – *a disaster was happening! it must be stopped!* – I ran from his car and hid in the hedge until he left and she went inside.

Then I climbed an outhouse wall, closed my eyes, and jumped.

When I woke, it was to the first single bed of my whole seven years: hospital ward in a distant city to which three men came bearing gifts, none of them my father.

First. Man with a beautiful beard who smacked me one day when he woke bad-tempered from a nap. He brought me a painting of a hamster; I let it fall and break.

Second. The one she wanted who wanted her back. He brought me a stuffed toy, before turning all his attention on Mother and what she had suffered.

Last. Him. The one I feared. Old and ugly to my eyes, whose few jokes were always at my or Mother's expense. Who would bring sweets for me, as now, then steal them back and laugh when I cried. Man who'd promised me the first holiday of my life only to leave Mother and me sitting for hours in his hot car while he made sales visits. Who was carrying me now – against the nurses' orders – to a metal sink in a side room so Mother could wash the dried blood from my hair. Where, although shy to be seen naked, my skin betrayed me by humming with pleasure at the water he poured warm against my back.

'That was like having a dad.' What I said when he went, forgetting why it was I'd hurt myself.

Mother in love with that middle man of three – what a relief to me. While they were together, I could slip free of her flannel, her rules, her need of my body in bed, and be what I wanted: a pony and its rider; a maker of mud pies mixed with chicken eggs; her admirer, his.

Because it was me who chose him – or so she let me believe – when we'd gone up to a chemist's counter in another town one day: him framed by the old wooden dispensing hatch just as she had once been in the bank.

I hid behind Mother's skirt and looked up at the man in the window, greedy for detail: soft dark hair, a funny moustache, deep voice, kind eyes, shirt and tie. How hungry I was for one of our own who wasn't Father, Grandad, a rarely seen uncle. 'He should be your husband,' I told her, going away, loud enough that he heard and soon after asked her out.

Silly, thrilling. What love between one adult and another looked like to me, witnessing it for the first time from wherever I could watch without being seen: the back seat of his fancy green car; through the flaps of a large empty box when he moved house.

Constant movement, wide awake. Running into the sea; riding horses; driving fast with windows down while he swerved against hedges for her and me to grab at grasses.

Fun from nothing. That too. As when he stripped to his underpants after work one day, letting her dress him in a tiny T-shirt and flared ladies' trousers for gardening clothes. How they rolled on the grass, laughing at his belly bulging out. The daily *Love Is . . .* cartoons he cut from his paper, doodling them rudely, so she would never let me look at the nude man and woman as I wanted. Nonsense I was excluded from, just as I was unable to read the shorthand entries she began to smile over in a diary I could always find but never decode.

She kept secrets from me in that short and timeless season,

but her beauty became looser, lusher – a late bloom replacing the pressed-flower memories of her younger self. Instead of precise rituals with buttons and brooches, her breasts bounced around under worn-soft vests, and her shoulders went freckled from days on the beach with him, just as she'd enjoyed with men in the time before me. She did cartwheels on the sand, handstands. Played rounders, Frisbee.

Wedged between rocks, I willed myself invisible for her sake and his: I'd overheard them talking – she was his first love; how he wished he'd met her at a different time when they were both fully free. He would be kind to me, but didn't think he, child-less, could ever feel himself a father, and me his daughter.

When she told me they were going to marry and move to a city far away, I felt the weight of me lift from her life, and hers from mine. *Yes, yes. Of course! And they would come back and visit?* Because I could not, having no father, be parted too from my granny, and friends, and new teachers . . .

I should have married the man I loved and made you come with us.

You should have married the man you loved and let me live with Granny like I wanted.

What we said, each to each, in the years that followed, when it was too late for either of us. Whereas he – childless, with a good job – soon found another beautiful woman to marry, and was happy, we heard.

AFTER THE FALL

What I tried to stop by jumping from the wall, I brought about instead.

Once home, the old man was our only visitor. But the kind-ness he'd shown while washing me in hospital belonged to the sentimental gestures he kept for the ill, the old and animals.

In closer quarters he seemed to me only an ogre, without a tender bone or funny one, who came to us twice a week for huge meals of meat placed before him, while my accomplished mother, for reasons I could not then understand, began to serve and sit, watch and wait. Always so fastidious till then, and still so in housekeeping, she began to smoke as he did, lighting each cigarette from the last; the atmosphere in our rooms, his car, became unbreathable. The ashtrays smouldered and a yellow smell coated our clothes, her fingers.

They married a while later but there was no honeymoon period. As soon as he moved in, savage unhappiness broke out: each of them using words for weapons and our poor stock of china as grenades and punctuation.

A GIRL IN PIECES

I woke one morning after a very bad night in the first month of their marriage to find Mother lisping like a little girl, and my stepfather a nervous boy fumbling to make me a breakfast.

Stop being silly. I shouted at her. *Stop it. Stop.*

But she only simpered again, saying she was so *tormented* that she didn't know who she was, or me. *Was I her friend? When was Daddy coming to fetch her?* Furious, and sure she was playing a game to frighten us, I shook her, then hit her, then pleaded. But nothing I said or did brought her back.

I was nine, and it was the first time I'd ever washed and dressed myself before walking down the hill to the bus – she'd never let me before. And by queasy coincidence it was a photograph day; I submitted to a dinner lady brushing my hair against its grain, and hated her, and the man behind the camera, and my dear teachers, and all my friends, for not seeing what my life was like. My own face, too, I began to hate, even before the picture came back and was put on display: a child's mask stuck on a body so old and tired that everything hurt.

No one knew, no one noticed, that my self split in two that day. Only I saw her go – a shadow slipped away down the lane – before I went back to the bungalow and whatever version of Mother was waiting there.

And this was how I lived afterwards. A divided child: digger, dreamer.

There was a sturdy girl with the face in the photo who went to school like a man to a mine, or farmer to his field. Education as a manual labour, through which – lesson by lesson, year by year – I'd tunnel beyond home and town.

It was a belief in the benefits of relentless effort already laid down at five when my first fond teacher of many, suspecting a cleverness rare for there, handed me a pyramid made of words while my classmates stumbled over *dog cat ball*. I said them all and knew them too, except the one at the top.

'*Uni–vers–ity?*'

'Yes! A faraway place, a bit like a castle, where . . .' she stopped to pop a toffee in my mouth, '. . . people like you who have worked hard to pass exams live and sleep and read books.'

This became now my direction and destiny – the only route out of that sleepless and unhappy house I could see for myself. But it was cold comfort, and a slow road to safety. My other half, the one I left in the lanes between home and school each day, wished only to lie down and wait for the man who would save me.

Sleeping and Dreaming

GOLDILOCKS, SNOW WHITE, SLEEPING BEAUTY: fairy stories of deep passivity which held no interest for me at three, four, five became now at nine my shadow self's obsession.

Oh those observed girls, discovered in their beautiful repose by bears, dwarves, princes! Watched over by candles held aloft. Tucked in. Left quiet. Woken with a kiss.

I traced them, again and again, with love, with envy, in the desolate times when I could not be outside or in school. What drifts of paper I filled with failed attempts to draw myself in their image.

Only ever interested in the mechanical world until then so that my few first toys had been trucks and toolsets, now I asked for dolls, just as other girls were throwing them aside. In my last year at primary, I pretended at my classmates' new interest in school discos and music magazines, while only wanting to be safe with my Sindys, my Barbies. I braided their hair (Mother had always kept mine short), stitched them clothes. Begged my gruff and only grandfather to build me a huge doll's house, taller than I was, which I minded with wifely care, back turned to the home I lived in. Things in the bungalow might get broken, and smell now of cooked meat, cigarettes and my stepfather's aftershave, yet in the rooms I owned everything was tended and intact.

But the problem with such urgent childhood fantasies around love and domesticity (as with too-particular sexual tastes in adulthood) is one of *reciprocation*: the impossibility of asking anyone to play along. With no one to know of this need to be seen and saved, my internal geometry grew fractal through force of longing; it spiralled in on itself, hoping for less and less. I wanted to be found like a hedgerow flower, or to become a field, a tree, its blossom – anything of use and beauty that others would be drawn towards.

My body, with its big and lopsided ears (legacy of Father and then my fall from the wall) – this I wanted only to escape through metamorphosis, like the nymphs in Greek myth.

And so the only tenderness I ever received from a boy – which came in that last year of my early childhood, sudden and unrepeatable as grace – this was of course decisive, enough to shape forever my sensual self.

It was my tenth summer and the quiet middle brother of a family new to our hamlet had found me lying in a cold frame, where I'd composed myself with a posy: Snow White in her glass coffin after the poisoned apple. I'd no hope of being found, was only enjoying there the warm air and my soupy self-pity. And so it was a thrill beyond imagining when he lifted the lid and climbed in, lying with me for an everlasting afternoon, stiff as corpses both, kissing until our lips went dry and cracked.

It feels like a single memory, luminous as dream, but we did it often after that for a while. A game of our own.

One day, he stopped kissing with his eyes closed and pulled back for perspective. He was *seeing* me. What I longed for, and yet shame made me flinch: painfully aware of all I was without – a father, freckles, ponytail, curls – I tried to bring him back close. But he used his free hand to stroke the side of my face, and then my already strong eyebrows and the delicate skin of my eyelids that even Mother never touched.

'You were once a Japanese princess,' he said. My fists clenched, ready to fight. He traced my cheekbones, one then the other. 'You have beautiful eyes, is what I mean.'

Some near time later he got or faked a taste for torture, and queued up with the rest of the farm boys who bound me and their sisters before twisting our wrists, our nipples – mean-spirited sex play that was my only reliable source of male attention before him and for a long while afterwards.

But he did, without knowing it, leave me a seed from which my love of art would grow. After him, I had an appetite for richer material than my old fairy tales as well as a hunger to know more about Japan. I begged teachers for books, searched old issues of *Reader's Digest* at jumble sales, and sat rapt a few years later through *Shōgun* – a TV miniseries in which a shipwrecked English sailor sat learning words from an exquisite painted lady.

There were no bright colours in any houses of my childhood, nor galleries or museums to visit: the only objects adults around me valued for decoration were glasses and plates kept in the china cabinets everyone had; my only glimpse of costumes beyond school clothes and farm wear were got at local pantomimes and carnivals. And so I came to my strange love of a distant culture only in this accidental way, from hoping to attract a man, and hold him in my spell. But eroticism and art cross-pollinated, so that whenever I had my hand between my legs from now on – other newfoundland that summer – my fingers moved to an idea of me in elaborate dress, neck bent over a drawing or book. In these fantasies I was always waiting for a boy but I began, too, to flush at the idea of being admired more widely for possessing some unusual skill – calligraphy, flower arranging, the pouring of tea.

To anyone who asked what I wanted to be when I grew up, I said *teacher, lawyer, doctor*. But what I really wished for I held fervent and close. One day, somehow, I would become geisha-like: a woman making beauty from the ordinary day.

§

But moments of grace – of being seen and let in – were far and few in those last years of childhood.

Before my eleventh year, I'd often seen my father but only in a passing, unplanned way if he called in on Granny Shadrick, his mother, when I was there too. There was no shared custody ever or even a regular visiting plan in place for me. But now he wanted my company each Saturday morning: his wife had a new shop job and it was a chance, he said, for my small half-brother and me to start spending some more time together.

He gave me a tour of their council house, explaining how everything was different, better, than the bungalow he and Mother had built: instead of cold lino there were these dark, patterned carpets; white enamel baths were from another generation – he'd put in this green suite, avocado-coloured. He saved the living room for last: a six-piece suite in brown velour and an electronic organ. How much I wanted to sit at the keyboard and try its many buttons. But I was there to play with my brother, he reminded me, which I did so that Father was free to dig the garden and tinker with his car.

One day, while cleaning out the shed, he put a chainsaw at my feet.

'All I was given after my father died so sudden. Your uncle had the farm, and all I got were some broken bloody tools.'

An outpouring, then, using me as Mother did.

He had wanted to bid for a lovely cottage soon after the divorce, but no one would lend him the money (Mother's old boss at the bank must have talked to everyone), and he'd been promoted now to senior mechanic but could still only afford a coach holiday to Norfolk once a year; meanwhile, his brother's farm was going up and up in value . . .

On and on, counting his losses and forgetting the time, so that his wife was due to return soon from work. He rushed to serve me lunch, and went back to praising his life at the expense of mine. My stepmother's cooking now.

'Puff pastry. And not from a packet – she makes it herself. Better than the rock-hard sausage rolls Granny bakes for you, isn't it?'

This I would not swallow. With fists balled tight, and standing for emphasis, I spat my food at the carpet.

He returned me to his mother and I was never let back into his house or invited to join him and my half-brother in any outings. As before, so again: my only encounters with him were accidental at Granny's, or brief sightings of his car passing by in town. Sometimes he'd arrive at the back door of the bungalow when my stepfather's car was away, wistful for the life he'd shared with Mother before me. ('*Don't you want to speak to Tanya?*' What she asked him once, as I listened, breath held, behind the kitchen door, instinct telling me to stay hidden until called. *No, it was only her he'd come to see.*)

After the worst rows in Mother's house, I would look sometimes at his name and address in the phone book, imagining welcome. But a perverse courtesy stopped me ever knocking the door, calling his number or asking for help. Self-control became a straitjacket; I feared being refused, and also what might break loose in me if I ever showed my need for love and rescue.

Only one more glimpse of a different life vouchsafed me back there, back then.

A boy arrived in our small, rural comprehensive like a swift, a swallow: golden-haired, flute-playing, fluent in four tongues; clothes washed soft and strangely cut compared to the shiny nylons from the market stall that I and my other classmates wore.

His family, we learned, were staying at an old manor house on a remote stretch of road between all the villages, and while they were in residence its outdoor swimming pool would be open. I was not then or ever in the crowd whose parents allowed house parties, nor would I have gone to one if asked: the strain of my double life left me (once the playground games of primary school ended) no easy, common language with anyone my age; I hid in the library at lunchtimes, and spent weekends mostly alone.

We'll be in the pool all Saturday afternoon. Come over. Said only to me one morning register, instead of the girls to whom everything happened.

Excitement. Then misery over the nasty bright swimsuit which was all I could find to replace my outgrown one when I rushed to the town's only boutique. Wretched sense of how different I looked to the girls who I believed would be there.

But I went anyway, cycling fast – mad with joy and singing aloud – down lanes I didn't know, to arrive at the large open gates of the manor. Which is where I stopped and could not pass.

What in my mother carried her so far and no further, I found in me too. I belonged with them, these children of teachers who would be going to university as their parents had – the surge of energy and purpose that carried me there told me so – and yet I turned away at the asking, the entrance.

Hiding my bike in the hedge, I found a place where I could watch unseen, all afternoon and evening, so that when he asked me there again I would arrive prepared, wearing the right clothes.

But that was my only invitation, and the year after that was his last at our school.

Boys, like men, I decided, had a painful habit of changing their minds. Removing themselves from view.

I spent the rest of my teens wandering lanes, cycling miles and sleeping for hours in far-off woods: *passing time* but wanting also to create conditions in which I might be found.

There is a torpor often in adolescent girls that has them drift to the edge of safety. But in my case, that hormonal pull was coupled to an even darker drive: the risk of being hurt now in my outside time began to beckon, almost. On an overcast day I might be heavy-bellied with dread at having roamed so far from home; on a sunnier one, baking myself by a tree or a river, my spirits would rise with daydreams of relief: of being set free through accident or emergency – a car crash, an attack – if I could not be saved by love. Anything that would remove me from my self and situation.

Fission

THE LONG, DARK SPELL OF CHILDHOOD: what broke it.

The eighties had just ended, and my mother and stepfather – still together, always at war – were united only in their drive to build houses and sell them: gold rush of that time. With the bungalow sold first to finance their gamble, they'd moved us to an awful rented cottage in a still more tangled web of lanes near nowhere. Such a strange, self-harming choice for Mother, that crumbling structure, given her need for what could be kept clean, and controlled. Ancient cob walls crawling with spiders; rats nesting behind the boarded-up bedroom fires; ants making a dark moving carpet across the floor whenever heavy rain drove them in from outdoors: so much dinge and dirt had a dementing effect. There was not a single day in those years when Mother didn't cry over that house and the husband who had led her there; and then I would weep too when the overspill of all that angry sadness swept my way.

That particular midsummer morning, their latest conflict had been going on for hours already.

With no nearby friends to visit, I went to the tiny next-door post office. I would take my time choosing penny sweets, then study the covers of every last video in the rental rack. Wait there for the noise at home to burn itself out.

But the ancient postmaster, his elderly son and their several women customers stopped talking when I entered, turning towards me like a strange arm reaching out to gather me in. It was unpleasant. Without precedent. *Was I in trouble for some imagined theft?*

'Oh you poor maid. How awful this is for you. We hear all the swearing and shouting, you know. It never stops.'

In their stupid, offensive tenderness, they made the sound of hens, clucking.

And to be pitied and pecked at by those decrepit old villagers? It broke me.

Back when I first cleaved apart at an unbearable situation – child aged nine, in those early days of Mother's new marriage – I became only passive. A digger and dreamer in which everything that mattered to me was sent inwards and underground for safe keeping until the distant time when I could *go*.

But now, at sixteen? It was cellular. Atomic. Triggering in me an energy release like a mushroom cloud, lifting me high and clear.

I let rip.

'So you hear it all, but not one of you has ever come round to say anything? What fucking good is that to me?'

The much-puttied glass on the post office door didn't shatter when I slammed my way out, but the awful spell of dailiness did.

It wasn't normal how I lived. It never had been.

The house was quiet when I got back to its front porch: my stepfather's car had gone and Mother was back-turned at the washing line in the orchard across the road.

How much I had always wanted to save her.

All those daydreams of finding her a better husband, or becoming one of those freakish children who make their family's fortune through a talent for song or acting.

And I could go across to her now and say: *Let's pack and close the door behind us. Start again, just you and me.*

But I knew she wouldn't come. Although she'd never spared me a single painful detail of life with that man, there was still some dark and labyrinthine logic to their marriage, and why she stayed in it, that I couldn't discover.

I went inside, seeing everything anew and for the last time. How ugly it all was, and my bedroom most of all. Plasticky-brown carpet and pink walls – leftover stuff got cheap that would do for me, my stepfather had said. At the window, heavy net curtains that had become part of that day's row – I'd pushed them aside to look at swifts nesting in the eaves, as I was not supposed to do.

In the long years since my stepfather's arrival in our life, I'd had a room of my own – what I longed for as a small girl made to lie beside Mother in bed. But deep and easy sleep had remained out of reach, the fear of being a woman and child alone replaced by the greater terror of arguments in other rooms. Through the worst nights, I would lie on the floor against my bedroom door, making of myself a barricade and sentry guard both, dressed in my day clothes in case this was the time I'd need to run finally and fetch help. Other times, I'd steady my wild pulse by imagining the sirens that warn of nuclear war (we lived near a coastal radar station that would be among the first targets). A total emergency as my chance to go: what an awful form of self-soothing, I saw now, to be comforted by what to loot and where to hide.

But it made packing to leave such a natural thing, having practised in fantasy so long. I was quick about it, unsentimental – beyond a few bits of clothes, there was nothing of use or beauty. The objects in my granny's house, these mattered to me very much, having been in their dear and familiar places my whole life – but here? I'd long ago trained myself not to care for them: all at too much risk of being boxed up or broken . . .

My racing bike in the shed, that *was* precious – bright red means of covering leagues each weekend – but I left it. I needed to feel every step between there and my grandmother's house, and I was determined to leave dry-eyed and soldier-straight, iron in my spine.

Mythic distance, those five miles in which I was *walking away*. Lanes pedalled along for years so I knew the name of every bungalow and the whereabouts of each barking farm dog; these passed into legend now, one that I was writing, by foot.

Then I set my gaze ahead, to the future, planning the jobs I'd need and the funding, to get lodgings near my sixth-form college. But as soon as I arrived at my grandmother's house to find her out, I reached as well the end of strength and self-invention.

Laying myself on the lawn like a baby, I fell into such a deep, immoveable state that Granny on return – despite being shepherd-strong still – couldn't rouse me. And so with a farm wife's instincts she simply improvised a tent from candlewick bedspreads and bean sticks, then left me there – under eiderdown – all through the night and next day.

A decade of badly fractured sleep began to knit and mend. But the harm to soul and self I was left with? That was another story.

Bride

The married couple sleep calmly in their bed,
he with his palm on the hip of the wife,
and she with her palm on the hip of the husband

Look! We Have Come Through!

HE WAS THE MOST BEAUTIFUL BOY I'D EVER SEEN, and there he was, sleeping in my single bed. I sat on the floor – throat still raw from coming hard and calling out – drinking in his skin, his smell, his shape. No other living thing had held me in a spell like this since earliest childhood, lying beside calves in my grandfather's cow barn: their sweet malted breath, dark curls, long lashes. They suffered my attention in return for licks of salt from my outheld hands; what, apart from sex, would keep Nye with me? Every time felt like the last: heartburn of happiness.

We were still in our first month of lovemaking, meeting every day after our shifts as summer cleaners of the university's vacated student rooms. We'd part ways at three in the afternoon to shower off the dirt of other lives, before getting messy all over again in my room or his bower-blue one, homely as mine was not (he had a trunk stocked with his mother's homemade cakes; the patchwork blanket on his bed was knitted in part by his Polish grandfather as a going-away present).

Neither of us was able to get enough of what the other embodied. I, to him, was a girl unlike any others he'd met in the three years of his degree just finished: bare of make-up, nut-brown from all my hours alone in fields, refusing offers of cigarettes at break times so as to sit separate with a book; it was a discomfort in my skin and social situations which appeared to him, looking on, as its opposite: beauty, confidence.

Him to me: so quietly at home in his bones, his clothes – a single pair of brown corduroy trousers, faded denim shirts. Listening more than he spoke always, head to one side and smiling, while the loud local women who supervised us tried hard to flirt with him.

When he finally asked if I'd like to do something one weekend, I said I was happiest outside: *Could we walk?* And we did, me leading him a merry dance six miles across the Downs in a heatwave before choosing some woods to stop in. Where I lay then, eyes closed, feigning sleep, girl become fox, waiting for him to decide if and when and how to get hold of me.

Afterwards, when I stood naked to shake out my dress, he was at first hunched over, shy to be seen the same way. But then he stood too, and straightened, chest expanding in a pantomime of male display; it was – he said later, laughing, as we went back along a lane confetti-thick with thistledown – an Adam and Eve feeling. The instant in which he cast off an overlong boyhood.

But now what? How to reconcile myself to the loss of his company? Because he would wake up, and these suspended days would give way to September when his real life as a new graduate would begin elsewhere, not here. At least the shortness of our time together meant he needn't know my real self: girl full of fears and phobias. It might, yes, be enough to have this one summer so close to someone so good, who would leave believing I was too.

§

'Welcome back.'

Kind-eyed Nye, sitting against the door of my tiny student room that was as bare as his was beckoning. Beside me, where I lay in sheets gone damp and sour, was a washing-up bowl, a towel, some untouched water.

'That was hard to watch. All day and night, like you said it would be. I only left a few times – to fetch food, use the loo.' He answered questions I was too ashamed to ask. *How long was I out? How bad was it? Did you see?*

We'd been walking arm in arm across campus when it started. Migraine. Adult version of my childhood white-outs, which laid siege to me after each of Mother and my stepfather's occasional incursions into my new and hard-won life of peace and quiet. I bent double, telling him please to get me fast to my room and leave me there. I was going to be sick for a few days and it would look and sound horrible. Really. He must go away. I didn't want him near me.

Our lovers' work of learning one another's childhoods had already begun, but I'd been careful to keep most of mine back, while enjoying how simple and sweet his was to me: scar below his knee from when a bottle of his mother's homemade ginger beer exploded; how he'd been famous at school for his huge hair; that he formed his idea of a right life by watching biblical epics – *The Ten Commandments*, *Ben-Hur*, *Spartacus* – populated by brave women, decisive men.

In return, I'd told him about Granny Shadrick, my great love. How her hearing aids let off a deafening shriek when she took them out each night. The strength she still had from years of farming, so she could beat men at arm wrestling. Her skill at making do and mending, and my own strange passion for household maintenance and repair.

But now he'd seen me ugly, broken.

'You were talking a lot of the time. Crying. Somewhere not here.' He climbed in beside me and stroked my hair that was stringy with sweat, even as I tried to push him away. We'd been together less than a month and I already knew I wanted never to be without him. But he hoped to travel for a year, and who would come back to a mess like me? He was though, as a parting gift, allowing me to lay down my sorrow a short while. I hid my face against his chest and spoke . . .

Of how it was to be a small only child down a lampless lane with two adults made blind and deaf with misery.

That I'd often slept against my bedroom door as if I could stop with my body the sounds coming under it, and woke still most mornings on the floor, however cold and hard the surface.

That the strain of that life – such unhappiness at home and the relentless study needed to one day leave it – made a social life impossible: I had no easy way of being.

That I'd fallen too far and too fast after leaving home so young, living in one unsafe place after another: doorless caravan in the woods that did as staff quarters at a remote hotel; a kitchenless flat of squat conditions; the basement laundry of an old people's home, where I ironed clothes and tried then to sleep while residents cried in the night for their wives, their husbands, their mothers.

That I only knew how to love men who were out of reach, and used sex to soothe my nerves, going with boys I didn't like just to feel met, briefly, on the wild outer edge of myself.

That I had, a few months before, ended a pregnancy.

That I'd just failed my first year at university, this escape route I'd been imagining all my life.

That I wanted only to return now to Devon and my granny's home, and live out my days there as an invalid.

And knowing all this about me, he would, of course, be going now and I wanted him to: because I couldn't do this after all, keep getting deeper in love when nothing could come of it . . .

Go. Go. Go. Using my fists, my feet. As I had just once before in my life, despite a horror of causing hurt: lashing out one day at the cows who came to my call in my grandfather's fields, because their quiet companionship should not have been so dear to me. The violent strength of shame: how it repels solace.

Go. Go. Go. And he did. But returned later and left a note.

*Your room, the whiteness of it, the simplicity. You telling me
you couldn't stand to just hang around one summer then*

watch me go. Me, transfixed by real conversation at last,
heart thumping with potential. I never wanted a life where
things went unspoken, where feelings were held back.
That's how I grew up – in a family happy to stay on the
surface. I knew what I was going to choose as soon as you
sent me away.

He came again and I let him in.

'I think you'll need to be loved for as much time as has already passed before you're free of all that. But what amazing things you might do afterwards.' What he said, that young man, just twenty, his voice holding firm after my flash flood of sadness.

And I should understand that he was happy to gift me his health and his steadiness, if I would teach him always what I learned – because it was not only me, did I see, who grew up with strange ideas of what a life could be? He had yearned from ever so young to know about art and books but, after seeing his father endure the miners' strikes, chose sciences, computing: compelled to have the best chance of a safe wage. And there was, too, a laziness in him, a complacency, which longed for my drive and determination.

Whatever plans we had for our lives before then, we put aside that day. Taking stock of what we were starting with – my single shelf of books, his grandfather's trunk, less than nothing in the bank – we began soon after on the pattern of our next five years. He began his first job and moved into my little student room when his tenancy ended, coming back each evening to the cooked meals I prepared for him. We ate from plates on our laps, with our backs against the single bed and my studies spread out around us.

Virgil, Dante. Eliot, Pound. Larkin and Murdoch. Hughes and Heaney. Sexton, Plath. I read from them to Nye, and he read back. We copied out hundreds of passages I might need for unseen exams and he tested me over and again until I got them all by heart. I wrote my essays and he proofread them. It was urgent that I pass with the highest possible marks – jobs in my field being harder to get at than ones in his – but for the first time I began to feel joy in my work. Going magpie-like through biographies became our shared passion: how Lawrence made a home with Frieda from each rented cottage by distempering the walls, sewing lampshades; the way Woolf and the rest of the Bloomsbury Group remade arrangements for living and loving; what it cost women poets of my mother's generation when they dared to voice their sexual selves.

We were learning through those late nights of our early twenties (so we believed) to go beyond our class, its constraints, and design a life of our own.

Playing Safe

I STOOD IN THE TOILET CUBICLE of a London train station, gagging at the dog shit caked on my cheap pair of ballet flats. It was the hour before my first day at a successful new television production company, and there I was with cleaning things begged from unfriendly Underground staff. Trying to scrub off the stain, the smell.

When this failed, I set off – blind with tears – into the unfamiliar city and its labyrinthine streets, aware of my life echoing Mother's: in the late sixties during the lead-up to decimalisation, the bank sent her to London for a coveted month-long training placement but she had a panic attack, catastrophic, just outside Paddington and returned to Devon on the next train home.

History repeating. I must pull myself together. Fast.

'Shoe Lane is just up there, love.' A stallholder setting up, when I said what I needed to find, and fast.

'Oh thank you. Thank you.' Only to find a joke had been played. It was an old part of the capital now made over to finance and the media, and any cobblers the street had been named for were long gone.

And so I arrived at work in bare feet, having to confess what had happened. It didn't matter to anyone else, or my prospects – I got my first pay rise after just a few months – but it was a bad omen that confirmed my fear I would never fit in.

The nights of study with Nye through my degree years had earned me the keys to a media career that we'd hoped for: graduating with brilliant results, I was offered – despite my milkmaid's accent, rustic way of dressing and lack of contacts – every job I applied for. Doors to big and beautiful buildings were held open, but I chose a small firm up a stairwell on a side street. Obscure, unthreatening.

How welcome I was made there. How unable to reciprocate. *No, thank you. I can't come to the launch, your supper, that party. I must catch the five-forty train to the coast.* This and other excuses until, as at university, my colleagues gave up, stopped asking.

And when I understood what little was required of me, and how fast I could do it (a pitch for a documentary could be done in an hour and justify my week) I drifted still deeper into difficulty. Pretending at research, I spent most of each day riding the Tube and hiding in libraries or archives, sitting among old people who smelled of medicated talc and ointment.

In that first graduate job, so long worked towards, this incredible boredom of being paid to do almost nothing stopped my watch, the world; I kept checking my wrist, the computer screen. Time as drying paint. One freezing lunch hour, I stood in a courtyard at the Barbican watching a maintenance man put undercoat on fixtures and fittings, and I was gripped by a forlorn, orphaned wish to join him. Then a terrible idea took hold, so my heart began to panic like a bird against my ribcage.

What if I'd educated myself beyond my nature?

And all this learning was only an awful mistake?

Me gone away from my place and people for *this*: little bits of paper turned out in minutes which kept earning me more praise and more money, so that I travelled up from Sussex day after day, unhappy somnambulist. Absolutely unable, given my working-class upbringing, to simply quit and risk a bad reference.

How much more I'd always enjoyed the jobs I'd had *before*, being a waitress, a cleaner, a care home attendant: using my body, my hands; moving through each shift in a blur of physical effort and easy talk with those I served.

I'd studied my way into error.

'You must just make time, Tan. Get up early. Go to bed late. Write before the working day.' What Nye said when I mourned how I'd never felt further from the writer's life than when cranking out proposals for programmes on scrap hunters, dog trainers, business gurus, clowns. Reality TV: this new genre that was fast stripping ordinary people of their dignity.

'We can be the shoemaker's elves, love. Make exquisite things while everyone sleeps.' It was a matter of time, of effort, as always.

And in this way, we began to rise together at five or first light (whichever was earlier) and write before the train: everything we could remember from childhood, as if we might, through pen and paper, recover all we'd each lost by going away for a higher education. Pages and pages on how our elders dug, built, knitted, farmed. Descriptions of the rooms we had moved through: china dogs, biscuit barrels, horse brasses, fly papers hanging from the ceilings. On and on, for no audience but each other. Until the only story Nye ever wrote.

THAT GOOD NIGHT. It was just an old Welsh man (a little like his beloved gone grandfather) walking home late and full of whisky through the steep terraced streets of a whole life. There was no action, other than the pensioner's unsteady steps, a glimpse through a window of a girl grown old, some poetry whispered by a boy who helps him when he falls. But it was also *the real thing*, and we knew it. Its publication soon after by an established literary journal seemed natural but when a BBC radio producer got in touch soon after to say they'd seen it and wanted it in a week-long series on new short stories by Welsh writers, this we *did* feel as extraordinary fortune.

Taking a day off work for the broadcast, we sat like excited children on the floor of our grubby rented flat, the radio held between us like a new pet that might bite our hand or run loose through the room. Such stomach-lurch hearing Nye and the story be introduced, but then we began to breathe, smile. It was beautiful, moving; imagined, true – *our ordinary lives could be art too.*

But after this little run in the creative world we'd both always dreamed of joining? We turned inwards, away. There was no big rejection or other emergency to explain it. Only a hesitance to leave behind our people, fully and forever, which is what we believed writing would mean for us. A betrayal, a severance. And so – being already so geographically distant from everything we'd loved in our upbringings – we simply went so far, and no further. We stopped describing our elders and began instead to live like them: a sort of incorporative magic, which our families indulged. Nye was allowed to have his grandfather's shoe polish and brushes; I carried away candle holders, fire irons, crochet hooks, sewing baskets, garden tools. It was a kind of playing at house and history that let us hide from feeling always out of time and place.

What relief, then, when my university offered me a way back soon afterwards: a job in which it was my task to run visitor services and attract more working-class scholars like myself so that, like my mother in the bank before me, I was – from my first day and for years afterwards – *walking on air.* Just as she had, I loved my name badge, my desk, my letterheaded paper. It was the best kind of play, of performance, to be paid to tell the story of campus and myself as a student there.

The only thing missing for Nye and me now in our mid-twenties (or so we told ourselves) was a home of our own, and this we found soon after marriage on a single day of searching in which we looked at just three terraced houses, the last having cupboards full of mouldering food left behind by long-gone tenants.

Despite the stink, the disorder, we found ourselves checking every room, each feature, as if it were a newborn: *See the old wood panelling under the stairs! The little lean-to beyond the living-room window – just like his gran's!* The back door to it was locked, so we lifted the sash and climbed through to the porch.

That hot plastic smell of his childhood, mine!

We had to have it.

Whimsy. Fun. Instinct. Lightness. How some of the best – and worst – decisions of a life are made. Walking over a threshold and seeing a stranger, a set of rooms, and emptying one's head, one's pockets. Taking a hand, a key. Exchanging the milk cow for the magic beans. Thinking not of cost or profit. Refusing the call of future possibilities that will fall away when choosing this place, that person. The way it is done: from smell, sound, stomach; all the senses coming together to assay the moment.

Every spare hour we had found for the writing life, we gave over now to the removal of wallpaper, carpets and ceiling tiles, before eating soup cold from tins and reading by candlelight for the months it took to get the electrics made safe. Sleeping happily on a mattress on the floor surrounded by the strange confetti made by all the debris.

Work and home began to balance, and when either of us in a rare empty minute felt the lack of friends or our old literary ambition, we trusted to the future. We were young still; that time would come again.

Shadow Side of Bargains

'WHEN ARE WE GOING TO HAVE CHILDREN?'

Nye's question breaking the quiet of our New Year's Day alone at home into sounds wild and discordant. A pigeon sobbed on our chimney top; outside, a child took a stick to the railings.

He'd put his book aside to look at me. Expectant.

I watched the light curdle and the small space between him and me separate, split. We were side by side in our ancient horse-hair armchairs that disgusted everyone but us when I bought them in my old home town just hours before we married at twenty-five. *Like yesterday*, I thought, while realising, all of a sudden, that for Nye it may seem otherwise. *A very long time ago, and too too much with just me for company.*

Very slowly, reluctant suitor, I got down on one knee and reached for his hand while my dry throat tried to make tongue work.

Is this how our marriage ends? I did not say.

'When are we going to talk about it, Tan?' Tears in his eyes, a catch in his voice. 'I've always wanted this, since I was a boy myself. To be a father.'

You are that for me, who never had one. This, too, I did not say.

'I've never wanted to have a small person in my power,' I said instead. 'What if they felt trapped, like I did? I've got no *model* for family life, no *feeling* for it. It's only something I wanted to escape. And what if we have a child and each stage of its life

80

triggers memories of what I'm trying to forget in mine?'

'But I've loved you ten years now. When will enough time have passed for you to be over all that?'

Never, I thought.

But instead of that terminal answer, I asked for *just a little longer, please*: if Nye and I could both cast off our inertia, our shyness – if we booked holidays and went abroad like normal people instead of spending our annual leaves parked by our childhood beaches reading books with our feet on the dashboard – if we began to use our money instead of only saving it for accidents and emergencies (his carefulness a legacy of growing up in that mining valley during the strikes; my caution got from the short rations of Mother and me alone) – if we lived more in our bodies and less in imagination – then we could try for one.

This time next year. Yes?

Like the miller's daughter who promises her firstborn child to a stranger if he will spin straw into gold, I did not think we would change very much, or that Nye would hold me to that moment.

Before we kissed on it in the white light that revealed his age and mine, I should have remembered the shadow side of bargains: their strange insistence on terms. Even when those who make them have no belief in fate or design themselves.

§

Five in the morning, very soon afterwards: our landline ringing. We sat up in bed, looking at one another before answering, knowing it to be the too-early time of births, deaths and accidents: Nye's family or mine?

Nye picked it up, then handed it to me. Eldest boy cousin on my father's side, whom I hadn't seen since my wedding day four years before. Our darling granny was not dead, but had been found on the floor in her bedroom, and as the only girl in the family they thought I should know . . . and perhaps start off in my car now and come stay with her a while?

A week later, I waved her off to a psychiatric ward – that beloved woman, whose house was the home of my happiest memories.

It was thirty miles away, the place that would take her; she had moved less than ten in her whole life: from her birth farm to the one she married onto and then, when she was widowed, to this little bungalow on the outskirts of town with its necessary view of sheep.

Once the car was out of sight, I buckled under the weight of guilt and grief, before crawling like an orphaned animal into her damp rag of a bed that I'd sat beside in the first broken night, and each that came after.

She'd been trying to die, she told me over and again, as I'd held her hand through every frantic waking spell. At first, she lay in wet fields, hoping the cold would do it or that cows would come trample her. Then she waited by the fast main road trying to get hit by a cattle lorry. The night before I came, she tucked herself in with photos of all us dear grandchildren and great-grandchildren – *did I see?* – and took pills. Kitchen knife; something electric in the bath: she would have to try those next, but hadn't wanted anyone to find her after that.

I believed her. Like the animals they managed, farming folk from that almost-gone generation did sometimes despatch themselves once their health and purpose left them. It was a refusal of leisure or infirmity at the end of a hard-working life that I'd learned about on childhood walks and Sunday drives: *That place there is where they were found*, Mother would say of a river, a garage or cowshed where an older person had drowned, or shot, or hung themselves.

Would I help her do it? Asked like a sly child in a sudden calm during the second night when I got her back to bed after she tried to stumble yet again from the house.

Yes, I will help you, I promised. Just as she swore to stay next to me every weekend bedtime of my childhood, only to pad back out to her fireside once the anchor of my leg on hers had slipped away in sleep.

Last wild minutes of that long week. Things I said and did before we left her house forever:

Fetched a best outfit so nurses might recognise her value.

Held up a mirror while she did her lips and cheeks.

Brushed her white hair as I'd never been allowed to do.

Sat her dressed and ready by the unlit fire.

Tried next to make a going-away bag which could carry the whole house, its essence, off with her to hospital: knitting needles, wool, wedding photo. The cheap beads she put on over a clean blouse every evening (a habit of *changing off* after each day's work to feel beautiful for her husband that she'd kept up all these years in his memory). Letter her favourite grandchild wrote from the farm in her first year of widowhood, asking if she'd please come back to help with lambing? The photos of me and others she took to bed on the night she tried to die.

Ran after that through the only remaining rooms of my childhood (Mother moved often after I left home; my father's house – that one painful season aside – remained locked to me). Rifled every drawer and wardrobe as if I could steal and keep safe how I loved her: cotton reels; shoe polish; jars of home-made jam and pickles; hat for chapel; fifty-year-old crêpe-paper Christmas decorations; smelling salts. Even heavy things I could never use, I wanted to take away in my arms: crank-handled sewing machine, coal scuttle, meat mincer.

Looking, looking, looking. As in the memory games she would make on a tray for my preschool self, whipping off the tea towel and daring me – *quick!* – to remember everything: *thimble, nutmeg, queen of hearts.* This time trying to hold her whole life in my mind. Soap and flannel by the kitchen sink that she used for her strip wash at dawn each morning. Sand timer got from a jumble sale with a crude drawing of a cockerel on the wooden board that held it, and this wisdom: *The cock does all the crowing but the hen does all the work.* Binoculars with foxed lenses and a mildewed case used daily to keep watch

83

on weather coming in from the coast towards the fields of her old farm.

Understanding, only then, how strange and static my way of living had always been. How I began when young, through loss, to prize routine and everyday objects more than people. As if by loving a person in pieces, through pieces, to pieces, I could suspend time, stop sorrow.

Last words. Me kneeling, holding her hands in mine.

'Have a good rest at the hospital, Granny, and be home for spring.'

'Once I go, I shan't never come back.'

'But you must. I'll have a baby before the end of next year.'

What I'd always pushed away, I now pulled close. An offering made in desperation to the woman I loved who'd been happiest in the care of children and small animals. Wanting – too late – to make a baby that would make her want to live.

A Frozen Landscape

TWO SLOW YEARS PASSED after I returned from my grandmother's house, asking Nye to come inside me, quick.

A baby: the very thing he believed would enliven us and I only hoped might transfuse my grandmother's last years with joy and purpose? Trying for one had led us instead to what felt like a frozen landscape, so that we struggled in those first years of our thirties to rise and start the days, dulled by the deep fatigue which sets in when a beginning or end will not come. Huddled under bed covers, backs turned on one another, even our rich married language began to recede. We tried to keep moving, and I even kept a diary of our days as we got closer to treatment, as Arctic explorers do on their treks – but what an insubstantial little record it made: all our attempts at talk and action like matches being lit and extinguished, one after another, in the hope that our courage would (this day as it hadn't in the days before) catch, kindle, sustain.

ROLE PLAY

'Pretend when we met you'd known about my crap sperm,' Nye said, once our doctor had confirmed it. So we did a role play in which it was our first walk again, and he told me and I didn't care.

But I *did* mind, although not for the reason he or anyone else might have guessed. Before the test results, I'd begun putting great private effort into a different kind of imagined scenario: one in which I freed him – with grace and generosity – from the burden of both me and my infertility (Nye's mother, mine; neighbours, colleagues: everyone just assumed the problem was me, and I did too). And while I loved Nye as I always had, I was certain now I had none of the strength or stability to be a care-giver; nor did I have the interest, only ever having wanted the equality of love between consenting adults, rather than the state of unreason I felt existed between so many parents and their children. And so I practised the tearful, relieving scenes – for him and me both – when I would say it was time to separate.

If I'd got pregnant in the first months of mad anguish after putting Granny away, I might not have regretted casting aside my lifelong wish to be childless.

Now though, I'd arrived at the worst possible scenario: having begun trying for a baby only to save a woman who couldn't be, I was heading fast towards painful and expensive medical proce-dures to become a mother, fully trapped by concern for my Nye. This kind and constant boy who made me a life-sized promise in our first month and kept it: how could I refuse him a chance at becoming a father? And if I did leave, what were his odds of finding a new partner who'd be prepared to have IVF?

No.

He had pledged himself to me, and I must be all for him. So I filled in the forms and insisted on quick referral times, pouring great energy from my small reserves into the one thing I wanted least.

TRIP OF A LIFETIME

Once we knew we'd be having treatment, and that we wouldn't need to pay for a first attempt, Nye said I could choose anywhere in the world to visit before the needles began.

But my fear of what was outside my so-small circle of the trusted and known meant I had an almost medieval mindset, the globe in my head being largely uncharted: *Here be dragons.* Only Japan had ever compelled my imagination, but I felt faint with terror just thinking of it: the planes and trains we'd need to navigate, and everything in a fully foreign language, without even an alphabet in common.

And so we spent our money and freedom on just a few days in America, where I went straight to the New York Public Library, asking in person for what had been refused me several times in writing before I flew out: that I be allowed to sit with one of Virginia Woolf's original diaries.

The most senior member of staff came out and told me *no*, and for the *last time*, saying that all the diaries – *as I must know* – had been transcribed now and published, beautifully. There was no need for anyone to read the originals any more.

He realised his mistake at the same time as I did, and I used it as my entering wedge, my righteous sword.

That is why I was there. To see the ink on the paper, I said. *To learn if it ran richer when she wrote of writing, or Leonard, or her love for other women.*

It wasn't true, of course: I only wanted to sit with one to know I had, and to have her rub off on me.

But it didn't matter that my lie had been invented, then and there, before his eyes. Its logic was irrefutable. He smiled at it. I was let in.

And knew, as soon as one was placed before me, with its fragile pages of unreadable script, that my idea of a mystical lineage was a nonsense. Touching that diary would in no way make me into a writer, any more than living on the Downs near Woolf's last home had helped it happen. Only my own stories risked on paper could ever do that. And if the IVF worked, the time to try again would be years away now.

What a fool I was: to take such a long journey for that unpleasant lesson, so quickly understood.

TIME, THE REVELATOR

'What will we do with all this time if a baby doesn't come?' Nye asked in the month before treatment started, another long and quiet weekend ahead of us.

Sitting with knees hugged to our chests, we were made children ourselves by the idea of so many years to fill now with nothing but work and leisure. It was as if – Nye said – a nursery child playing intently at shovelling buckets of sand was told: *You won't be allowed to outgrow this like the others.* Suddenly then, the thing that was fun would feel like a punishment.

COPING STRATEGIES

Last weekend before treatment.

How I sat late evening in the red armchair beside Nye's, begun upon a crochet blanket, new pastime by which I hoped to *control myself* and *stay put*, instead of running away fully and forever as it was now my urgent wish to do. The wool was orange like the binder twine Granny and other retired farmers used to fasten their gates and fences, and I tried to imagine myself likewise bound to my seat.

So restful, you knitting like that. What Nye said several times, even while my fingers whispered for me to throw open the front door and set feet free. But I knew what I'd see if I did: bright circle made by the last lamp on our small street – and beyond it? A dark in which I'd belong nowhere, to no one.

Old knot of fear and longing. Girl awake through so many country nights, too scared to run along lightless lanes and reach the help she needed.

How stuck I was still.

Whereas Nye, meanwhile? Intent on growth. Our tiny house filled by him with seedlings so our rooms had a new and thick greenhouse smell; every surface covered with trays and pots.

His trouser pockets full of loose seed now whenever I emptied them for the washing machine. And such close attention he bent towards those plants – little, multiplying substitutes for the child that refused to take root. I offered to share their care, but he shook his head always, and continued alone.

Back turned to me, our life.

Out of Time

WHENEVER WELL-MEANING PEOPLE asked after Granny or the fertility treatment in those years, I held my throat and opened my mouth without sound coming out. Voice stopped by my twin sorrows.

There was only one person with whom I could find words, and for the first time it was not Nye.

Yuri. Not his name but the one I gave him, he being part-Russian and with the old-fashioned look of Doctor Zhivago. He existed apart from work and home both; older than me and senior in one of the region's other big employers, we'd met on a monthly management course between his county and mine.

Those day releases had surprised me by being more about meaning and purpose than any of my undergraduate seminars or television writing projects. While the reason for our each being funded to study there was purely corporate – to make us better business leaders – it was my first chance to talk with others about personality, ethics, motivation. How quietly exciting it was to answer questionnaires then discuss the results in groups. Finding ourselves not only office workers after all, but *inspectors, advocates, architects, crafters, commanders.*

Of us all, Yuri was the least forthcoming always; not cold or cynical, only *self-protective*, I thought. A light irony used like a sort of matador's cape to keep his private ideas just out of reach.

The rare reserve Nye possessed, Yuri had too, and so I hoped for his good opinion.

In the second year of the course, I earned it, but only after failure. My particular difficulty (and part of why I'd been sent for training) was public speaking – something I was required to do, and at large events. But I never did it well, my breath going shallow and the audience becoming awkward, so that it was a misery for them as well as me.

And now my turn had come to do a presentation there. I felt my hands and knees begin to shake, and after just a few sentences it became clear I couldn't continue: the men and women with whom I'd shared so many easy classes had begun to study their shoes, their fingernails. *Such humiliation.* But then Yuri met my eyes, sending out a little smile as lifeline, before asking me a question.

Which I found I could answer.

Everyone was able then to breathe easily again, me included. And I found I *could* stand at the front and talk, so long as it wasn't me pretending to be an expert, lecturing people. Conversation, I could do.

You were awful . . . and then superb. That took courage. What he said afterwards, so that the fatherless stray in me, starved of praise always, got an instant hunger for more. But then the crisis with my grandmother happened, and on return to the course two months later after a missed session, I'd become a woman with a stone in my throat. I took my lunch outside and away from everyone.

How hard it was to care for ill relatives now that so many of us live so far away from them. What Yuri said, coming to find me in the far corner of the institute's gardens. Having spent much of his childhood in boarding schools on different *continents* to his father, a United Nations official, he now did long drives most weekends to care for a man who'd so often been absent.

Both a little light-headed on so much disclosure from him

so fast we put our sandwiches in the bin and went to a nearby pub for proper food: bacon, eggs, chips. Which became then a monthly ritual that sustained – courtly and decorous – even after the course ended.

The hours with him were chalk circles: fairy-tale clearings in which I was freed to speak. Sitting always a table width apart, never touching yet held by his warm attention, I could say how it had been to arrive at my grandmother's house and spend the first days cleaning her filthy kitchen instead of simply sitting with her and giving love, as I should have. How I left her alone in the next room by an unlit fire while I stood emptying stale biscuits and weevil-ridden flour into the bin. Shaming her.

Why didn't I give up work and live with her? Or bring her up here with me, against the family's wishes? A busy farmer when her own mother came to the end times, Granny had nevertheless found a way to give my great-grandmother comfort and purpose – sitting her by the stove, and handing over orphaned lambs to cradle, wool to unravel and wind. *How had I failed so in care, in kindness?*

Those were my shames. His were different, but just as difficult to live with. Boarding schools placed him in a *panopticon*, a prison of *total visibility and political intrigue*, when he was by inclination a deeply private child. Always with the wrong accent and idiom for wherever he was sent, he began to model himself on that character in *Peanuts* – the one obsessed with Beethoven: how he had been. Deaf to overtures of friendship, and hunched taciturn over his studies, as he was now at work (he used his fingers to mime the angry playing of a toy piano, which was also, he said, how he typed). After school, like me, he'd fallen fast in the world – out of his privileged caste and into bar work, labouring – until being saved by late-taken degrees and this job he disliked but would cling to till retirement. He was overpaying his pension to get the leaving date down, but he was still looking at a *twenty-year sentence*.

After a few months, he laughed that we should keep minutes

on the topics we covered: Buddhism, Philip Larkin, *Brief Encounter*, Laurie Lee – we kept finding more and more in common.

In a letter Nye wrote for my birthday just before the IVF began – when I was already in my second year of meeting Yuri each month – he had this to say about it:

> *What is hard for me about this need you have – as my wish for a child is difficult for you – is only who you choose, where you place it. This yearning for male love: take care, please. It has the smell of dead roses on a gravestone, your desire to lay yourself at the feet of older men. It would be different if any of them were better than you, or me, but they were only born before us.*

I was able to reassure him, and honestly, that the meetings were no threat to our marriage. Because when the course ended, and Yuri had continued travelling out to meet me, I'd found a way of asking. Moving the salt and pepper cellars about on the table – *he, me* – I wondered aloud (with more lightness than I felt): *What were we doing together, really?*

Ah, he had said. *Ah.* I was attractive to him of course, but he'd suffered terribly from his own father's infidelities. The impact they'd had on his mother, and him, and his sisters. And so he could never do that to his own wife and children – and he had sensed I was not looking for that either? That I was happy with Nye, but without any other close friends or family? Could it be enough then just to keep enjoying our shared taste for *really good table talk*? This thing done so well by men and women in the old films he loved, yet hard to find in real life?

Yes, I said. *I understand. I'd like that too.* And so we carried on with our courtly conversations. For me, who'd never had the attention of an older man, *it was enough*, I said, even though I soon found myself living best and most intensely in only those few hours dedicated each month to the seriously adult pleasure of thinking and eating together.

§

And now, after three years of these meetings, it was our last lunch before the start of my maternity leave (the IVF having worked first time). After Yuri had pulled out my chair and helped me, huge, into it, I placed a piece of paper on the table. *A parting gift*, I called it, being certain he'd never want to meet again now I'd always have a baby on my hip.

For later. What I said when he began reading it, but he shook his head and kept going – smiling, laughing – to the end. Looking at me afterwards in a new way, his colour changing, and then his voice when he spoke. A rare show of strong emotion.

Ah. You made them for us. How very beautiful.

I had. Ever since that early lunch when he'd joked about our need to keep minutes, I'd begun, in secret. Using the precise style of his organisation and mine, with only a few lines for each of our many long exchanges, they'd been done for comic effect, but were note perfect: becoming in this way somehow more than the sum of their parts; capturing and compressing – in that light way of oriental ink paintings – all that was good and strange in his imagination and mine. (And it was my first writing beyond private diaries, I realised, only in the moment of handing them over and seeing them read. *How thrilling.*)

I placed my hand on his, the first time, just a moment, fastidious as ever about his marriage: that circle he'd drawn around it at the start.

Do you love me, just a little, after all? No. I mean: Have I mattered to you? Will you promise always to remember me this way: a young woman in a lovely dress, just days before her child was born?

All I wanted to ask, I swallowed. Pretending a need for the loo, I went to a cubicle and bit my hand that had just touched his until my tears and need to plead for love had subsided.

It was over. My chance to be a childless writer like Woolf, Iris Murdoch, de Beauvoir, Nin. And these meetings with Yuri, and the small enchanted spaces in the everyday I'd made from them

94

– nearest to the life of art and beauty I'd always wanted.

I belonged to someone other than myself now, whether I liked it or not. This boy or girl in my belly: they would soon come roaring and wildly alive into the world after their dream-time inside me. And should I survive that arrival? My own life would ever after be in service to their needs before my own.

REINCARNATION

stripped bare

It is time to explain myself . . .
What is known I strip away

First Breath

AGONY OF SENSES.

An instant, violent, incomprehensible waking. How it is to be reborn.

What was I? Where?

I was blind: I could not see. Were my eyes cut out? And so bitter cold – was this a mortuary drawer? Or the surgical theatre, and the operation still happening with me able to feel but not show my suffering?

I was dumb: I could not speak. Was I split down the chest then and my lungs exposed? Declared dead in error and set aside unmended? Nothing else could explain this silent, sightless, butchered sensation.

My name being said, so that I rushed to my own eardrums, those only parts of me still working.

'*Listen.* We had to leave the pipes in. You may go into cardiac arrest. So you must show us you can breathe on your own. We know it hurts, which is why we do this so rarely. Three breaths. As fast as you can.'

This was how my second life began.

With fear and hurt so raw, so vast, that I learned what torture is: when you don't die of pain that is unendurable, that might only stop if you do what unknown others insist you must. And in doing what is compelled, part of you that has been wholly and unassailably your own, inviolate till then – it shatters. It spills. And can't be gathered back.

I forced my lungs outwards, up – *once, twice, three times* – and was delivered of the knife in my throat.

My heart withstood the shock. Life support could stop.

But those breaths after surgery were posthumous: the me of my first thirty-three years – that girl, that woman, who had worked so steadily to keep herself hidden, safe and small – was dead. My new self was stripped bare and spreadeagled; flayed too of consoling ideas about how life might be kept neat and tidy.

I'd seen a light that contained an immensity, in which every leaden error of human nature had been burnt away. A place where souls had slipped free of self and could meet and merge, guiltless and promiscuous: that close contact I'd been yearning for since earliest childhood.

Whereas here, now?

What a cold and lonely planet I felt myself returned to. This world, and myself – how metallic, how tinny. And my biography that I'd begun to shed with compassion and relief in the ambulance – a torment now, to have it back, like a can tied to the tail of a cat.

My son, when they placed him in my arms that were still pierced by needles and bound around with tubes, was likewise an assault on me. The medical team smiled at the sight of us reunited as if we were a nativity scene. Them as the shepherds and me a Mary, mother mild.

But I wanted to hand him away. And shout. Protest.

How could I be expected to come back and bed down in the narrow role of a new mother, confined by this one suckling newborn, when I had so briefly touched the universal? What kind of wife could I be now I was pulsing with a new need to go alone through the world, pure soul, free spirit?

And where love for my baby should have been, there was nothing. When I gave him to Nye before the operation I'd sent the current which ran from my son to me *away, away* to his father. At the level of energy, I cut myself off so he'd flow towards a connection that would hold.

But now I was back, against the odds, and changed. I felt no tenderness, only the constraining facts of my marriage, my motherhood.

I tried to say something of this then – to them, to Nye – and they all bent their heads and cupped their ears towards my mouth. But my throat was too sore, too swollen: they couldn't hear me.

Realised then, with animal instinct, and just in time, that they wouldn't approve of what I had to say anyway.

They might consider me a risk to my son or myself.

Trap me in a locked ward!

I must hold my tongue.

Nurse my wounds. Bide my time. Plan an escape.

My new life would depend on it.

Aftershocks

HE IS NOT A WIDOWER.

He is walking into hospital with clean clothes for a wife who is naked in intensive care, snaked about with tubes and on intravenous morphine, but awake now and breathing without a machine.

Light-headed with relief and lack of sleep, his thoughts bubble up, one after another.

The ring on his finger: it still has its mate, in his pocket for safe-keeping, but soon to be back where it belongs. He smiles at the idea of marrying again when his wife is returned to a ward and they can be behind a curtain. The way children play at weddings: yes, he will kneel beside the bed, and ask for her hand.

And she still has her womb, he having begged the surgeon to save it – not for another child, but so his wife wouldn't wake to find a life stage cut away.

How good it has been simply to shower! These have been his first hours alone in a fortnight of birth, surgery and now the three terrifying days of induced coma. Perhaps tonight he can rest: his mother has arrived from Wales to mind the baby and Maria, mother-in-law, is travelling up to be with his wife, who was stable when he left; hard to look at – lines in her neck, arms, groin, thigh, and a catheter coming out from between the legs – but good to hear, even husky as she was from the pipe that had been pulled from her throat. Telling him, yes, she could be left; that it was important to take care of his own self too: wash, eat, sleep.

An animal sound coming up the corridor.

Wild, high, horrific.

Unearthly, like the vixen in the field across from the house when a dog fox was stuck inside her.

Oh, someone suffering something awful. And without his wife's strong stomach for the body and what comes from it, he fears witnessing a stretcher going by with whoever has been mangled by car crash, knife attack, burst appendix.

But he arrives at intensive care to find it is his wife who is screaming, and has been – the desperate-sounding nurses say – since soon after he left. There has been an argument about it: they have defied the consultant on duty and are insisting the surgeon who did the operation return to hospital because this is *not normal* – the patient was stable, lucid, until she was moved to a handheld pump for pain relief, and then this happened.

The surgeon returns then, and watches a while. Asks the wife if she is having a baby.

'*Yes. Help me. Make it stop.*'

Ah. The stitch he placed around the womb to save it – a rare procedure only done at the hospital once before – has, he tells the husband, caused unnaturally fast contractions in her body which has already endured two abdominal operations. There is no threat to life, but she is likely wishing to die from it. He instructs the intravenous morphine to be reinstated and they wait.

Within minutes, she is returned to sanity, herself. Says, soon after – her voice eerily remote – that there is an order of pain from which nothing can be learned. It merely happens, and stops happening.

And you survive it, or you don't.

§

The paradox of accidents and emergencies: soul has rude awakening, wants to fly, but is tethered to a body reduced to its most basic and convulsing needs. *Sleep, shit, swallow, piss.*

As for my newborn son, so then for me.

My first day out of intensive care was spent on a commode being watched by Mother, my stepfather, Nye, a nurse. To perform a bowel movement was both important and risk-laden: days of opiates had made my insides slow and stinking, but I must *come on now* and work those muscles. *Stop holding it in.*

'Oh, I am the San Andreas Tar Pit,' I laughed, then cried.

The nurse went out, cross, and was replaced by a care assistant. Large, jolly.

'You mustn't come near. I smell of death. It's disgusting. I'm so ashamed.'

The woman leaned close so no one else could hear.

'Listen. I'm a children's entertainer in my other job and I've seen shit there you wouldn't believe. It will be my privilege to wipe your ass after what you've been through, so take your time and get it out of your system.'

Laughter, tears. Release.

Second day out of intensive care, I began – in a new and imperious voice – to question the wisdom of being handed my son for constant breastfeeds.

Was I not full of drugs? Weren't my breasts dry and empty? And his fingers were sucked raw. He seemed lighter, thinner than before . . .

I was told then the hospital policy of promoting breastfeeding over bottle: its long-term benefits to baby's brain, health, happiness; the importance to my bonding with him, too.

But wasn't my need to recover more important? And his to be without hunger? And how had he been fed when I was out, anyway?

At which I learned, with disgust, that had been a discussion about whether to pump me for milk while sedated: selfhood reduced to supply chain.

Fury, outrage.

Bastards!

I swore at Nye too, telling him to fetch bottles, formula – *lots of it, and ready-made, starting with cartons from the hospital shop –* and fuck anyone, family or nurse, who said another word.

It was not only love I'd woken without, I found then, a wild surge of strength galloping in my blood: passivity was leaving me too.

Niceness and compliance: childish things to be put away.

Third day out of intensive care, and the three of us were fully reunited in a private side room.

We flicked through the TV channels for some background noise, a balm. But it was all too bright, too happy. And so we turned down the sound just as Hitler appeared on screen, a puppet jerked about by his own rage and hatred.

'Look!' I said, pointing to our baby, who was spellbound. 'It's the black and white, the contrast – what newborns see best apart from faces. Quick. Climb in while he doesn't need us.'

Nye did as he was told and snuck in under the covers of the high-sided metal bed, only to send money from his pockets scattering loud across the floor. Outside, a person going by stopped, stood listening.

'Touch me,' I said.

And he did, there and then, despite the stitches, our baby, the eavesdropper, Hitler, and my body came fast and gasping to his hand, quicker than it ever had or would again.

My soul, meanwhile, sat apart in the corner. Unmoved by the lure of an easy relief, with eyes on the door.

Waiting to Escape

WE SPENT SEVEN DAYS IN THAT SMALL HOSPITAL ROOM, the three of us. And I confined still further, not able to leave it as husband and son could, so that the bedside locker became my fiefdom, my battleground – only external thing over which I had control.

How dare Nye or the nurses move anything!

I was angry with everyone. A graceless patient, hard to handle.

But my private thoughts – whenever I was given a few minutes alone with them – were not at all volatile. Rather, a deadly internal steadiness was settling in: my escape being meditated.

How should I do it? When?

Best, for Nye's sake, to make it soon, so that he and everyone who'd have to be told could agree: *She must have been more damaged by it than we knew. Not in right mind.*

I planned what to pack. The note I'd write.

But what about money? It was all in a shared account now, and this, I found, was my sticking point. What I could not contemplate.

Leaving Nye and our baby: this promised release to the horses charging wild through my veins and nerve endings – a cliff edge I could bring them to, after which they'd fall away into dark water. Into silence. Relief.

But stealing from that good man? Taking out hundreds, or thousands, of pounds just when Nye would need to give up work and care for our son?

No.

And if I couldn't afford to live, I'd have to find a way to die. Beachy Head, infamous local suicide spot, began to beckon. *Yes.* Once I could leave the bed and my legs could get me to a bus stop, I would head there. *Jump.*

Back in the last years of my adolescence – that solitary outside time – I found a sheep. Miles from anywhere, and tethered by brambles; fly-bitten, dead. But bending closer to look for a farmer's mark, I understood, with horror – of stomach and mind both – that she was *still living*. And all the grass eaten bare around her head so that she might have been that way *for days*.

I could have walked away. Told a villager hours later. Or not, letting nature take its course. But the sight of such entrapment brought me to my knees, and I began, barehanded, to free her.

Weak as she was, and thirsty, how she fought me.

Throwing her body hard around the few inches left to her so that the thorns pulled tighter. I put my face close to her face then, and tried to signal good intent. She submitted.

Hours it took. She bleeding, me. And the stink of her, the state: I was sick, several times. But the ewe – once her brain had let me in (*as what? a saviour? or only an unstoppable force?*) – lay there with the upturned eye of a saint. No external sign any more of pain, or fear.

It was dusk when I got the last hooks loose. I knelt behind her and made of myself a lever, wondering how next to keep her away from the undergrowth until I could get to a phone and call for a vet . . .

But the minute she was on her feet, she went away from me. Not a backwards glance. Veering sideways, starved and torn. But away, without hesitation, to wherever it was she belonged.

(Oh it is appalling what the body can endure. Its will to live, despite such damage. Our hearts lacking the rabbit's rare capacity to simply stop and spare us from suffering.)

SECOND COMING

body electric

Womanhood, and all that is a woman . . .
The voice, articulation, language . . .
Sweat, sleep, walking, swimming . . .
O I say these are not the parts and poems
of the body only, but of the soul

IT DOES NOT SUFFICE FOR ME simply to tell stories of extraordinary experience.

Ever since those first tales I heard from Mother, my passion has always been the study of cause and effect: what happens *afterwards, next*. How we change in response to sudden illness, oddly timed encounters, unsought gifts. Why so often we *don't*, refusing to let ourselves be shaken, or moved. Or we react, but in ways that serve neither us, nor others.

This is the purpose of my story, now.

So I will proceed then like an engineer. Steady, measured. Show how it was to return to the world, now that my way of seeing it had been altered forever.

And there should be no more surprises in this book – those storytelling devices of suspense and melodrama – beyond that rush of blood, the inhabited light, my terrified intakes of air.

I tell you plainly: *I stayed*.

And wanting to go but deciding to hold fast – this became a lathe and chisel shaping me in strange, new ways.

Our tales of awakening – told across the centuries – so often hinge on severance that it's hard to imagine lasting change without it. Castaway, cast out, or parting from a place and people, our heroes are enlivened by *leaving*. They set out, sail away, seek the wilderness. We are taught that only by freeing ourselves from constraints, or forgoing loving closeness, do we become tested, and testament. True to ourselves, example to others. Fully awake to our lives and times.

But I decided on a different path. To see what might be achieved by *staying*. Not like my mother and her mother, a martyr staked to circumstance. Nor as a disappointed woman, placing the weight of my unlived life onto a child.

What would it take, instead, to be a person alert to possibilities in the everyday? To find, or make, new ways of living around – *even through* – the role of mother? To be a quiet pioneer inside the confines of a small town and my middle age?

At the start of my second life – despite being the weakest and most frightened I'd ever been – I chose *effort*.

Not the resigned kind of my childhood, always striving towards the distant time when I would have passed enough exams to get the job that would keep me safe.

This was a hardier variety, and more hopeful. Infused by that vision of a more generous life I'd glimpsed during the near-death: the sense of a great, collective energy wanting me – *quick!* – to come out and play.

But as soon as I did achieve a bright new way of being?

I tunnelled under it. Blind mole, turning towards darkness and testing to destruction all I held dear. *How, why.* These axes on which we plot our lives even as we proceed – as I did so long – wholly or half-asleep to them.

Mother

go freely . . . with the young and with the mothers of families,
read these leaves in the open air every season of every year of
your life, re-examine all you have been told

Unsought Gifts

THE MINUTE I CAME BACK to the tiny house I'd left head first on a stretcher, something was waiting for me there that had the feel of fate. The first of many odd events in my second life, it was tempting – then, and each time afterwards – to imagine a destiny was unfolding; that I was now in the hands of a force beyond my own small self.

Because how to account for the fat letter in a thick cream envelope that lay on the doormat?

Money from the estate of my late grandmother, that woman who'd lived on less than anyone I knew. Who wore jumble-sale clothes, and whose only sources of heat were coal fires, hot-water bottles and embrocation oil rubbed on to warm her muscles.

I'd already had an unnerving sense of her life force being lent to mine: she'd been dying finally ten months earlier on the very day I lay in a clinic, watching a screen on which an embryo divided from two cells into four. I went into labour on her November birthday. Now this. *Signs and wonders.*

Even stranger was the way the money became mine. Her old and cold bungalow on the far edge of a rundown market town: I'd always known it was left entirely to my father as late amends for the family farm given whole to his brother so long ago. And if she had died in the house, so it would have been: it was indeed willed to Father, who'd not be allowed to sell it, but only live there for the rest of his life before leaving it in turn to *his* son, my half-brother. There was no provision for me, the daughter, Granny having a landowner's fixation on male inheritance.

That had been the plan.

Instead, with the sale of the bungalow to pay for her care, a codicil was triggered in which whatever remained must be divided among her grandchildren. By sending her away from home three years earlier – that necessary decision I made because her sons could not – I disinherited my father, without he or I then knowing it.

And so now a share of that money had come to me. Enough to leave the country, rent a room, retrain: all the unaffordable ways to start again, alone and away from everyone, that I'd grasped for in the hospital and then set aside – so abruptly now in reach.

Yes, how to reconcile that uncanny cheque which provided me with the means to leave my husband and child, just days after the problem of funding my escape had left me contemplating suicide as my only way out?

I put it on a shelf by the door. My grandmother's death and legacy become my skeleton key to freedom.

The next unexpected gift came from Yuri.

My only visitor in the first week home, how surreal it was to have him – so remote from the rest of my life always – there at my bed's end with that air of a kind doctor in an old film I'd seen in him from the start. Smiling at me while I fumbled to change my son's sleepsuit, just as he'd watched me struggle with the presentation at the beginning of our odd relationship.

'Shall I do it?'

Of course. His children that I'd never seen – they were school age now. Everything new and difficult for me already nostalgia for him.

I nodded, made shy and also ashamed by the ease with which he did it.

He'd shown kindness, and courage, to come to our front

door and cross the threshold. Yes, it must have been a difficult, tender thing for him to negotiate when we'd only ever met alone at country pubs for walks and long lunches.

But something in his being there – making small talk as if I hadn't almost died only days ago – appalled me. Deeper than cosmetic shame at my clumsy new mothering and misshapen body, it was disgust that rose up: a too-near and too-soon reminder of the brittle, little ways in which I'd spent my time in that old life. *Oh what a minor, melancholic key I'd played about in.* Putting my creative energy into talk with a man more routine-bound than me even.

Once he was gone, I studied what he'd given me. A Joni Mitchell album. I searched the lyrics for a clue of what I was to him and found a mark beside a few mild lines about a man who comes for comfort, consultation.

It wasn't enough.

What if I ran away from all this – husband, son – only to continue mooning after older men? Could I really trust myself to live a richer, wilder life if I left? Fully free, rendering service to others? There was no evidence I could strike out on my own and thrive. Yes, I walked away from my mother's house at sixteen, rucksack on my back, but how far and fast I'd fallen afterwards. And in all that time since, Nye was the only person who'd ever loved me fully and without reserve: our bodies home to one another. What a shame he'd wanted this child I was not equipped to care for in the same way.

During the next fortnight in which I could only shuffle from bed to bathroom and back, head spinning with anaemia and my plans, there was no late hormonal flood of love for my small son as a miracle cure for my wish to bolt: our connection was still fully absent. I took beautiful care of him but he had no deep claim on me.

But the arrival of my grandmother's money *did* begin to produce an unexpected side effect: by providing funds for an escape, it also *bought me time to stay*. Perhaps because I felt less fully trapped, I could stop gnawing at *how* and *when*. Yes, I could afford now to wait a while. To help Nye through these first sleepless months, and see if I could master my fear in the meanwhile. Salvage some self-respect, at the very least.

How long would I need to give it? A year?

Terrifying amount of time to be in such close proximity to a child with its huge and exclusive need of my flayed mind and body . . . but if I could give that to my son before going, I would have at least shown good faith. And if I left then on the anniversary of my haemorrhage, who could blame me?

A broken woman who tried to mend, but could not: the note I would leave, when I did.

Flight, Fight

YEARS BEFORE, A CHILD STILL MYSELF, pregnant without meaning to be, I lay on hay in another country beside a newborn calf. I'd travelled there with a foreign boy who loved me, despite my situation. He simply couldn't bear that I would have been alone on campus during the holidays while (in his words) *waiting to end the mistake that I had done to made.*

His family were Catholic and spoke no English: there was no way to say what I'd brought with me, and so instead I ate food served in unfamiliar ways at an old oak table – trying to swallow small bites of rare beef while nausea rose in my throat – and straining my small stock of Spanish to show that I, too, came from land and livestock. That I was not the frail-seeming visitor of shamefully small appetite I appeared to be. *Mis abuelos tenían una granja mixta? Vacas. Ovejas. Pollos. Trigo.*

One day, my friend was asked to do some ploughing, and I sat on the back of his tractor, freed entirely of the need to speak for the time it took the sun to move across the sky. The progesterone of my still-early pregnancy quieted my will and worry; I was at home in my skin for the first time. Sleepy, smiley. A tilled field. I daydreamed of keeping the child, becoming a foreign farmer's daughter-in-law. Rising at five as my grandmother had, baking for the men, washing out the milking parlour, collecting eggs, plucking poultry: that cyclical existence which held her safe. Her soft gold wedding ring had rubbed through from all the feed pails carried across the yard over the years, and I wanted to be worn smooth that way, through use, instead of sitting neat at my endless second-hand study of other lives.

I was so lost at that time that I didn't then and still now don't know where I was that week. I look at maps sometimes in case a name will come back to me, but it is no place I can find. The happiest day of my first two decades, and I arrived at it as I left: sleepwalker in my own life.

Just before we were due to return to England and me to my operation, we were called to one of the sheds. A cow was stuck in her labour. *I could help, yes? Not mind?* And because I had seen many animals delivered, and chickens strung up and bled, I nodded and went in. It took three of us to free her of it, putting our full weight on a rope that ran up to a pulley and across the shed to the hooves sticking out from the mother's hind parts. Such unendurable force. The cow began to bleed and buckle, and so they sent me outside, where, soon after, the calf was laid beside me in the hay. A photo of me there survived to become a favourite of Nye's: long brown hair, green swimsuit, a girl so young, curled tender around an orphaned animal; what was growing in me, still invisible.

A week later, lying in a line of pregnant women waiting for our anaesthesia, the cow and the calf filled my mind, sudden as a shaft of light on an overcast day: *I could accept the foreign boy's offer to marry me. Keep the baby and raise it in fields like the ones of my childhood.*

Just as I decided this, the girl next to be sedated after me began to cry and struggle. *She couldn't do it. Sorry, Dad. Sorry, Mum. Sorry sorry sorry. Would they take her home?*

She left, and I stayed. Let it happen, a mind and body divided.

§

Strange, what can decide a life.

That memory of a baby I didn't have years ago. How a

120

potential shared future with that unborn child was ended by me on a single day, choosing control over possibility.

Who was I to escape responsibility always?

And by what right could I sentence my son to the awful emptiness that comes from missing a parent? That hungry ghost sensation of my own childhood, got from Father's retreat: could I inflict it on a child in turn?

Another consideration, too.

If one soul-shaking aspect of my near-death experience had been this wild and driving wish to slip free of self and live more expansively, the other had been a painful awareness of my first life's cowardice.

A double bind, then.

Or my challenge?

To make motherhood my first measure of courage in this second life.

No, it had to be more than that.

Something in my spine straightened, as it had when I left my mother's house. A bit of me that wouldn't bend to the idea of being only in service to my son. Impossible though it seemed to change my own life while also attending to his all-consuming needs, *I had to find a way.* I couldn't afford to wait until he was in school, or grown and gone; this thing in me newly awake – that appetite for greater connection – I couldn't risk putting it into hibernation for an easier time. That was how my first life got lost.

So. To stay, then, and not in a self-abnegating way but with style, and purpose, balancing somehow the scales of him and me. Become an explorer of the everyday and break new ground in it.

Who is the third who walks always beside you?

Line from an Eliot poem I was rereading in the aftermath of Yuri's visit, which spoke to my painful, shameful longing for more male love; this offered now a vision of how I might push through my fear when alone long hours with my son. It was, I already knew, the poet's mistelling of an eerie experience had by explorer Ernest Shackleton and two of his men in the Antarctic when they trekked a day and a half through killing conditions to fetch help for the rest of their party: only much later did they confess each to each a sense of another person walking by their side until they reached the safety of a whaling station. It became, through Eliot, a phenomenon known as the *third-man factor* – a feeling, by those near to death or despair, of a preserving angel.

My son and I were in that degree of danger: the risk of a new mother from a difficult childhood developing postpartum depression was high, as was the likelihood of me suffering post-traumatic stress disorder after my time in intensive care. And, since the operation, I'd been left, too, with a burning nerve pain that made it mechanically hard for me to move. So I was anaemic, crippled, frightened, and soon to be a baby's sole carer between the weekday hours of six in the morning and seven at night. Our odds of doing well together were long.

Yes. If I was to keep going, I would have to be my son's fellow explorer and our guiding spirit at once. An immediate lifting of dread told me I was, in my laboured thinking, getting close to something saving. The terrain of my motherhood, certainly these early post-operative winter months, would be wilder, bleaker, than for many. And I should approach it that way: as an expedition, in which there was no room for any excess weight. So all the maternity guides that were causing me anxiety before his birth, and everything my mother-in-law kept telling me to do against my own instincts (swaddling tight, avoiding eye contact so he'd sleep), and what the few mothers I'd met months back in prenatal groups were determined to do whatever the cost to themselves (breastfeeding for the first year, co-sleeping): over the edge it went, like the dinner services and silverware early polar explorers abandoned on the ice.

Our survival kit would be composed of no received ideas

– only food, shelter, cleanliness and warmth (of skin, voice, gaze). I would learn him, and he me.

I was still terrified of being left all alone with a baby, but now I felt determined, and yes, a little excited too. Because hadn't I done this before, as a child? Sent half of me ahead up the lane, while my other part trekked slow to safety? And mad as it would sound to anyone if they knew, how did it matter what moved me so long as it was felt by my child as love?

I emptied the little nursery of childcare manuals and baby magazines, and restocked it with true stories of endurance, endeavour: books I'd bought compulsively over the years, but never bothered to read, as if just having them to hand would make me braver, by contagious magic. Scott's diaries. Thoreau's. Walt Whitman's *Leaves of Grass*: that epic celebration of the body, free love and free-thinking – a set text from long ago that I'd only skim-read then, finding it too alarmingly far from my own cramped sense of self.

Made then a base camp out of blankets and pillows at floor level where I could manage best with my bad back. Carried up a flask, our wind-up radio, candles, cartons of formula, nappies, and food rations for me.

Went back down, panting with effort and adrenaline, and asked Nye for the baby. *I need to be alone with him now until I go through my fear and out the other side . . .*

Then, over my shoulder as I went up, a grim little joke to show I was not mad or manic. Only attempting heroic stoicism, in the style of Titus Oates. *I'm just going upstairs, I may be some time.*

§

Most new parents prefer their child asleep. In repose, eyes closed and quiet, a baby is a sweet, good thing, easy to love.

But now I needed my son awake. On the floor in the far corner of his nursery, with a draught from the window coming in, I stripped him, then me. Nappy, maternity pants, nursing bra; each tiny movement of his limbs and mine making pain flare where I'd been sliced and stitched twice over. Next, using nail scissors I couldn't imagine taking ever to his unpredictable fingers, I cut us free of the plastic name shackles put on at the hospital (left on so long through my fear of rupturing again).

And there we were at last: two naked animals, wide-eyed and facing one another.

I put my lips to the soft place on top of his head where smell pulsed strongest. Nosed at him, but still nothing moved in me. *Birth cries, hot skin; the metallic tang which triggers recognition:* all this was missing between us, even before the still more violent separation that came later with the haemorrhage. Delivered by emergency Caesarean after a two-day labour, he'd arrived still and silent, and was taken away from me out of view. When placed in my arms long minutes later, he was already blanket-wrapped and wiped clean of his messy, necessary scent.

He struggled now against my chest that was not his father's, and began to fuss.

Panic, self-disgust. I was not what he wanted.

I laid him away against my bent knees still better to see each other and began to sing. It was only, at first, for myself: a whistling in the dark, for courage; a way to ease my unease. But his body began to respond, tensing and turning about in search of the sound, so that I tuned myself to him in turn, making with my face each shape that passed across his, my song modulating as I did. If his hands spasmed closer to mine, I brought them to my lips and kissed them, still singing so he'd feel the hum of me against his skin. When he made a noise, I echoed it. In this way, through a sort of whale music, we floated free from clock time, our culture. Began, unobserved, on the depth work of becoming mother and son.

Through the Looking-Glass

HOW UNREAL MY SMALL TOWN APPEARED when I could at last walk free from the house in the cold new year, months after my return from hospital. Four in the afternoon and almost dark by the time I had us both bundled against the chill each day, I pushed my son through streets that had the off-kilter quality of bad dreams. Bright and beautiful, but having a glassy aspect: blind to me, resistant. Tudor-fronted shops spilled light and promised heat, but had doors too small to attempt with the buggy.

Motherhood was not only a state of mind, I understood, but also *a place*. I would be raising a child in these particular streets and so I needed to find friends in them for my son and me, shy and atomised though my way of living had been until then.

For the first few weeks of our afternoon walks, the only people who ever spoke to me were pensioners, who stopped to stroke my son's new skin as if it were gold leaf they could lift off and use to restore their own. And so, face burning with cold and shame, I went eventually to the tourist information centre, explaining how I'd been too ill to keep up with my prenatal group. And so I didn't know where new parents *went*, what they *did* . . .

'Have you just moved to the area?' The girl at the counter smiled at first but went red as I was when I said *no, I'd lived in town eight years but had never spent much time there . . .*

It was true, though it sounded stupid, and was. Residents almost a decade, Nye and I had only ever browsed the flea markets and antique shops on weekends, or strode out to the countryside beyond, or gone around the stalls at summer fêtes, finding the stallholders funny, quaint. But really, the joke was on us. They had a *community*, which we were without. In the working week we'd both been in our offices, and during holidays away. There was not a single house in our town we could call on in friendship.

How humbling it was, then, to ask for an events listing and run my gloved finger along the limited options for new parents: baby massage, sing and sign, a weekly toy library.

Like a child in its first days at school, I began to watch out for other mothers. Where they went, how they behaved.

At tin tables outside the windy precinct's coffee shop, young mums with local accents gathered. I sat close by on a park bench, feeling clumsy, old. These younger women handled their babies with an easy rhythm I envied, guessing it came – as with the mothers of my childhood – from living among extended family. Little cousins or new nieces and nephews passed to them at gatherings, when they were still young themselves. They would never invite me over, I knew (even in my own home town, I'd had a bookish look that set me apart) but the way they talked was good to hear. I fed the jackdaws and pigeons, hungry for crumbs myself.

Some of the shops that sold small, beautiful things had cafés with a toy-box charm, and this is where the older and wealthier mothers met. How inviting these spaces were, like the cottages in fairy tales. Wooden chairs of many styles and colours, food served on pretty mismatched crockery. Sweets in glass jars. A stack of board books for toddlers to pull about. Low play tables with wooden trains. But women already in newly formed groups were always there first, prams and pushchairs circled like wagons. Breastfeeding or opening pots of puree while discussing home improvements, holiday plans, return-to-work options. They wore silver rings, had honeyed hair, seemed so improbably slim . . .

Here it was, old habit of an awkward child! To notice a few bright details in the lives of others and assume me both unlike them and unlikeable. Who knew what rips and repairs – to body, to mind – these women were nursing: there was no easy language for it, as I myself was discovering. I should not judge them on their table talk.

Yes, what a disservice to my son, this poor way of seeing. He would likely have no siblings, and Nye and I had no nearby family to offer him; was I only going to pass on my isolation? This sense of having my face always pressed against the glass?

My father's closed door, the unrest of my childhood home, all the house moves, the nerve-fray: this had made me an outcast. But like so many who feel tender and unsure, I'd pretended arrogance until it became me: scales on my eyes and a hard shell around self made from layer after layer of refused opportunities.

§

Graduations, birthdays, christenings, weddings: these official threshold events have photographs that help us celebrate and remember. Our small, private steps from fear into courage are rarely recorded this way, so it is easy to forget their importance. How life can be transformed by taking a breath and walking through a door on an ordinary day.

There is no photo that shows me pushing through the stiff entrance to a converted church one spring morning, come with my son to its playgroup. Finding a space among the toys spread out. Laying my baby on one of the mats, heart hammering, before making shy upward glances at others who had come alone.

A few familiar faces. Women I'd seen in clinics? At the supermarket? And over there – stranger with a cloud of dark hair who spoke to her boy in a calm, quiet voice I admired.

If she was on the radio, I'd listen all day.
I thought this and smiled.
She smiled back.
These simple exchanges that change everything.

Oh the relief of that time. To have broken through my first life's resistance to showing need or want.

And what a surprise to find – as we all began to sit together in the town's flower gardens – that they had noticed me before we'd met, even while I felt myself invisible. Just as Nye long ago had mistaken my reserve for confidence, so now I listened, astonished, to the other mothers' ideas of me: *My walker's rucksack stocked with bubble mixture and books: how organised I seemed, how disciplined at getting out each day. And what authors were so important to me?*

I dared to say just a little about the emergency, its effect. That the writers I'd read in my twenties hadn't prepared me for living after all, so that I was studying now those who saw the world through fresh eyes and shaped their days in the way I still hoped to do. Rumi, Rilke, Jung. And Whitman – him especially, his *Leaves of Grass* being now my articles of faith, always with me.

As for those women, to me? Steady, rational, generous. From childhood homes as stable as mine was not. They might so easily have turned away into a group that excluded me: that natural instinct to withdraw from anything strange. Instead, they let me be their mystic and bringer of odd ideas, sharing in return their family traditions that I was without. And in this way, like the sheep on the Downs around us, we began to raise our children. Together, in the open air. A shared attempt to make sense of our new terrain.

O Pioneers!

IN THAT FIRST YEAR OF MOTHERHOOD, we women had the air of people waking up late from a dream of equality.

Women with professions, me and these other mothers I'd had the good fortune to meet. But who were we now without our paid work?

It should not have been a shock to the system, our milk-stained shirt fronts, stretch marks and sciatica, but it was. Our educations had not been concerned with our bodies, beyond a few classes on the facts of life; we'd all studied since our teens through period pains, hormonal migraine, PMT. Earned our place in offices and institutions. *Now look at us!* How strange our male partners appeared in contrast: going about unchanged through the days, when we were now so cut about . . . and also *cut loose*. No one to answer to but ourselves.

How courtly we were, and determined, as we went to each other's houses carrying flowers, cake: we women who'd worked full time since graduating and had never been in our own homes this much. So romantic, for me, having grown up isolated down a country lane, to push off from my tiny terraced house that opened straight onto the street, and arrive at garden paths on more expensive roads. To bruise rose bushes and apple blossom with the buggy and stand in the perfumed air by doors with delicate leaded panes, waiting for the mother inside to finish a breastfeed and answer my quiet knock. Our calls, each to each, as a sort of cross-pollination: not only a passing of time until our partners came home, but the beginning of long conversations from which new selves would flower and fruit.

On first visits, there would always be apologies for kitchens that were soon to be rebuilt. We stood in these provisional spaces, babies on hips, learning each other's lives while turning about so our children's fat hands could not pull at cookbooks or pan handles. A strange dance of care-taking and talk. We continued to feel clumsy in the streets – obstacles to avoid – but when gathered together in a home or garden we practised competence, beauty.

We were serious, then. And shy about it – but only because being in earnest is never in fashion; ease always sitting more lightly with onlookers so that we learn to perform it at a cost to our real needs. But we none of us had safety nets, being counties or countries away from our own parents (those of us who had them still, which was shockingly few). We had to go slow and take care. Be painstaking as we patched together what it was to be a mother, a woman, from borrowed and remembered sources.

We were looking after new humans and hurting no one around us in the attempt, so how extraordinary to discover the dark side of motherhood in our culture. That what raising babies and small children in the Western world most resembles is being bound and gagged on stage before a critics' circle of family and strangers both. Older people tutted at us in public places, muttering about mothers and children today; men mostly found us distasteful and turned away.

Living between two worlds as I did – working class by birth, middle class through education – I soon came in for another form of censure. Neither Mother nor my mother-in-law made themselves available for regular help beyond that first emergency visit, but were scornful about my spending time with other women: it was breaking the law of generations on Nye's side and mine. There was an absolute taboo on visiting people to whom you weren't related.

'*Housing*, it's called,' said Mother on every phone call when she asked about my week and I told her. 'Not that anyone born and bred down here does it, only women from *away*. And nothing good ever comes of it: talking about private business.'

My elderly neighbours, local born, shared this view, asking – like Nye's mother always did – how I *had time* to invite so many other mothers and children into my little house (which was still kept like a neat pin, so it seemed self-evident to me that I had more than enough hours alone at home).

All this only made me more passionately convinced that my near-death vision of greater connection was the direction to head in, fast. Memories of unhappy women from my childhood now haunted me: those mothers of my few school friends. Always alone in daytime, they'd endlessly patrol their house or garden, calling one minute for children to lick a spoon or taste a carrot just pulled up; in the next, they might explode with rage over some mess or breakage. As a child, I'd been incurious as to their inner lives and keen to keep out of their way; now I wanted to return in time and recover them all, and ask: *Was that what they'd wanted for themselves? How did they bear it, all those lonely hours? What stories would they have told, if anyone listened?*

My new friends – most of whom had more educated mothers – tended to have milder memories, but I found them just as unsettling: the close oversight of their development; an anxious investment in music, dance and sports classes. The sense conveyed that they, the daughters, were all at once too much, too little, too necessary.

Whenever my son was feeding in the crook of my left arm, I had a book held out on my right. All the feminist classics which had held no interest for me in my twenties, I devoured now, finding confirmation in them of what a rigged game it had always been. Even the chapter titles were instructive: Greer calling out THE MIDDLE-CLASS MYTH OF LOVE AND MARRIAGE; Betty Friedan warning of THE MISTAKEN CHOICE, THE FORFEITED SELF and an insidious phenomenon by which HOUSEWIFERY EXPANDS TO FILL THE TIME AVAILABLE.

So I was quick to shrink it, instead.

I asked my neighbours if they'd meant what they said about taking my son out each day in his pushchair to the ducks? *Yes?* Then here was his bottle and dummy. *An hour would be wonderful and no, not to nap or clean, but to read or write.*

And I suggested soon after that we new women friends not only meet in parks or each other's homes to talk mid-morning, but that we could also make the grimly repetitive end-of-day hours better by taking turns to do teatime for all the babies and ourselves, while sharing out the housework too? (Begin upon a bold collective endeavour that might even endure into our old age, when we could pool resources to buy in care on our own terms!)

Yes, I was making it up as I went along, and there was an energy to it. A hum of rightness. Night-times were still long sleepless stretches that Nye and I did in shifts beside our boy's cot, but the days – always for me before a narrow field of study and then work – flowered now into a rich ecology of shared experience. And there was a chance, too, to cultivate new skills. Sewing, baking: so many practical activities my relatives had refused to pass on to me (saying *with your education, you won't need your hands*) I learned now alongside other mothers.

We were always tired and often bewildered. But it was a pioneer feeling too: building the village we'd need to raise our children.

Stress Test

I HAD PASSED MY GREAT TEST OF CHARACTER. What I began to think – in glowing communal moments and my privately efficient ones – as my son and I reached the end of our first year together.

Even more than my hours in parks and other women's homes, my favourite time became now the mild autumn evenings, when I'd sit on the pavement outside our little terraced railway cottage, son on lap, my back against the warm red bricks, listening for Nye's train going through the nearby tunnel. Watching then for his dear shape to turn into the end of the road and come close to lift our baby from my arms into his own.

Being alone with my boy had become easier than I'd dare hope, as well, and this was the most satisfying thing of all for a woman who'd got to her thirties without having babysat, or had care of a pet or plant even. To find that my hands held generations, and knew what to do: by which I mean that Granny and her talent for minding children could be summoned, reminding me that just a bubble made from the dishwater – blowing steady through my cupped, wet fist – this could stop a child from crying. That a button in an empty biscuit tin could be rattled to the same effect. As could walking my fingers *round and round the garden like a teddy bear* from my son's tiny palms to his chubby under-chins. Or peeping from behind a tea towel. And singing still all the time back and forth – me like a blackbird, him like a crow – so that I could move about the house and he feel secure while I did.

I still dreamed most nights of the near-death and its siren call towards a vast simplicity, and I woke from these always with that wild and driving wish to *go, go, go* . . .

But then my engines would turn over, my gears engage, and I'd move us smoothly through our days like an air hostess whose only purpose was to deliver my son and me to our new routines at work and nursery. My first life's love of order protecting me from the overwhelming muddle of motherhood my new friends said they struggled with: however tired I was, I followed an unquestioned routine of my own creation. Making the bed, the cot. Dressing us both in clothes put out in neat piles the night before. Packing lunches; washing the breakfast bowls.

As well as the blessing of my child's sweet temper, I was also cushioned by privilege: granted a return to work on three days a week when he was six months old, I had access to an on-campus crèche and was able to eat lunch with my son in the grounds, surrounded by a fascination of jackdaws, flowers, gulls. And I shared his care, once home, with a loving husband who was away in daytime but an equal partner in the handling of night feeds and wakings.

You've got it lucky. What Mother said often on the phone. And although I was always in pain, and never not exhausted, I agreed, while also inwardly congratulating myself on the drive and self-control I possessed that she did not. I was fortunate, yes, but also at *the helm of my life*, steering it now and not drifting any more, nor being capsized by storms of feeling as she had always been.

Yes, I thought, *I'm becoming wise to this business of living.*

But I was not, of course.

There was another rude awakening soon to come.

§

The pregnancy test was only a precaution before I went for an emergency CT scan. I'd just been rushed by ambulance to hospital with suspected meningitis, and a nurse insisted I be checked beforehand even as Nye explained about our IVF.

What a shocking positive.

And because it was not safe for me to have conceived again so soon, I had decided by the day of the very early scan that I'd ask to end the pregnancy, however much Nye would love another child. There was my constant nerve pain, and a tiny house already a squeeze for three . . .

And I was simply too frightened to begin again. To endure another haemorrhage. To have a new baby come between my son and me just as we were enjoying a closeness I never imagined myself able to share with a child.

I'd missed no period, I thought, waiting for the sonographer to wave her wand: it must have been discovered by chance in the very first days. There would only be a few dividing cells still – not anything over which to risk making my son motherless.

But what came into view instead was a kitten-like creature with two tiny paws held close to a cat-shaped face, smiling and somehow self-sufficient – already past the three months mark and anyway impossible to harm now I'd seen it.

I returned home to what felt like my grave-in-waiting; only a matter of time until the artery that tore before would give way again under the strain. And so – while I continued to pin my hair up in a neat crown of plaits each morning, and put on my make-up, and do office work and household chores – I began to prepare for death. In practical ways, as there hadn't been time for the previous year.

I wrote a letter for my mother, then Nye. Packed his grandfather's trunk with things of comfort for my son in a childhood that might still now be without me: the soft dresses I'd worn in these first and only seasons together, smelling of him and me commingled; his earliest sleepsuits and pyjamas; my diaries with the darkest parts torn out, so as a man he could discover the long-gone woman who'd delivered him. Telling only my closest new friend what I was doing, the one who just months ago was that stranger in a church hall with a kind voice and cloud of dark hair: *Would she stay in his life, please, and tell him silly little things about me as a new mother?*

Then, with my house in order – although not my heart or my courage – there was nothing to do but wait.

§

Two years to the very day I'd been discharged from hospital after the haemorrhage, I was delivered there of that child conceived as unwittingly as her brother was planned and procured. A coincidence of dates that felt like grace: a chance to return and repair the damage of that earlier time.

So it was. Pulled from me fast and easy, my daughter came into the world as loud as my son arrived quiet. Placed wet and bloody on my chest, our cord still connected, she rooted her way with fierce instinct to a breast and began to feed.

You made the sound of a happy animal when they put her in your arms, Nye said later. *It was bizarre and beautiful.*

That is how we were, she and I: strange, wild.

And alive!

I insisted then on a private room and holed up with her there, reluctant for even Nye to come close.

She was oily as a seabird, and dark as one, smelling of liver and kidneys – a tang of blood and offal I refused to wash off the entire time we were there so that everyone else held her at a little distance. Only I clutched her close, licking, sniffing. We were silent, unseeing; all of it done through scent and skin, without mind or effort.

It was a love affair lasting three days – all we'd have alone together in that lair I'd made before we had to join the top-world noise of my son and all his many friends. A beautiful interlude that I enjoyed without hurry or guilt, not mistaking the ease of her arrival for an accomplishment or happy ending. It was only good fortune. I knew now my real test of character lay in the months and years ahead: one baby might be tended into order; two could not. And so whatever I'd been hoping to do with my second life beyond work and home, but hadn't even begun to plan in any real detail? That vague self was now so far off in time and possibility as to be at vanishing point.

The Hours

SO TIRED SHE TRIED TO DIE.

What Mother had told me about Granny Shadrick's first and long-ago attempt to end her life. After the stillborn daughter, mother to two small boys, a farmer's wife with a flock of sheep and men to tend, after and amid all this, a day came when that woman full of laughter and love for her work *simply could not do it any more*. She forced herself up from the bed she'd always risen from easily and stumbled through still-dark fields to the railway tracks. Bit like a wild animal at the hands which discovered her before a train came. *Carted off to Bodmin then, the loony bin*, Mother said, *for shocks from electric and cold water*.

But also, I thought now: *rest*.

In that first year of my daughter's life, I had a single hour a week to myself. Nye insisted that I take it away from our tiny house, so I drove a few minutes to a quiet car park by the town cemetery where I could cry unseen.

An annihilating wish to go to sleep and not wake up had hold of me, which I confessed only in illegible notes kept locked in the glovebox.

I might have gone for a massage, a sauna, a coffee – things my other mother friends did in a rare spare moment – but what I wanted could not be bought.

I wanted to sleep long enough to heal my broken nights and ever-present nerve pain.

I wanted to be free of the recurring dream that would not leave my soul at ease during the fragments of sleep I did get. An insistent and upsetting scenario in which I'd find small children and the very old – like so many lost sheep – in the damp shadow of an ancient wall. Over and again, I'd lead them to a vast wooden door where the light of my near-death poured forth through the cracks. But when it opened, as it always did, I only ever handed my charges across the threshold. *Why was I crying?* an unseen voice asked each time. *There was room for me too?* Upon which I said my own fixed lines – *My place is outside* – before waking instantly to tears rolling down one cheek then the other.

How I resented it. My sleeping self's yearning to be rescued from difficulty by . . . what? God? To whom I'd stopped talking at four, five, already hating my hunger for a father figure.

What else?

I . . . (This is where my writing would rip into the paper. Savage disgust at being so *invalid*.)

I . . . wanted to live apart from Nye and the children – *any small rented room would do* – and come in to them at five and leave at eleven in the evening once the babies were put down. To be not a wife and mother but a *housekeeper*, their *nanny*. Yes, to be a servant, with days that were long and hardly paid but which *ended*. Allowing six hours of separation in each twenty-four.

But instead, life had become an insatiable engine into which everything in me got consumed, day after day, so that I felt like a stoker shovelling coal into the boiler of a great ocean-going ship. A season of inexorable forces: physical, economic.

My daughter refused a bottle as my son had not, so couldn't be easily shared about with neighbours as he had been.

Our house was so small that there wasn't room for her cot beside our bed, or by her brother's (she had to go in a Moses basket on the landing), and so my grandmother's inheritance had to go towards a larger house. No more private escape fund for running away or renting a room of my own.

And crippled so often as I was, but with no parents nearby to help, the only real carers for the children were the ones I paid for: even part-time nursery fees for two babies being so high that we could only afford it if I went back to work again once my girl was weaned. The office, absurdly, as the only place I might be relatively free to rest.

And yet.

At precisely this point – when the time I had to myself was reduced to almost nothing and the money of my own was gone – *this* is when the raw hunger for experience surprised in me during the haemorrhage reasserted itself.

How? In those car-bound hours, once I reached the end of tears and self-pity, I began to hold on to it as a thing in me hard as a pea, felt through all the layers of culture and convention that seemed to swaddle others from the passing of their numbered days. Disturbing my peace; a memento mori. A discomfort of soul that I chose to keep close so I shouldn't forget the terror of regret exposed in what I'd believed were my last minutes of living.

I accepted then that my second life was never going to be altered in the mystical way experienced all too briefly during the blood loss: that delicious *slipped skin* sensation, as in first lovemaking or finding oneself arrived finally to a great and warm welcome of like minds. But if the yearning to reach beyond my roles as wife and mother I'd been left with was still burning so strong despite everything – *and it was! it was!* – then I must treat it as my vocation, even though it didn't yet have any worldly form I could articulate to others. It was nothing I could hand over at the doors of a church, medical school or university; there was no clear course of study I could apply for and undertake in the way I'd given shape and status to my first life.

Instead, I would need to start navigating only from my own deepest instincts and values. Relax my infernal will, accept my obscurity and experiment with a more fluid way of being. Strike out into the unknown, with more energy than I possessed, and spend whatever few free hours I had as if I were rich in them, not poor. Become a spendthrift of time, not a miser. I, more than most, should understand by now the error of trying to save it.

Swimmer

Long have you timidly waded,
holding a plank by the shore,
Now I will you to be a bold swimmer

Those Who Are About to Die

ALL THINGS BRIGHT AND BEAUTIFUL in my second life came from those darkest hours in the car park, when I chose time as my teacher, and decided to apprentice myself to it.

This element in which we are all of us at swim or adrift – natural resource that can't be dammed for future use, or gathered back in (both of which I'd always tried to do, even as it ran through my fingers). And it occurred to me then that there was one place where my small, spare ration would have true use and value: *among those who had very little left*. People who were coming close to their end: they may have a thirst to speak frankly, and by listening I might meet my own need for a deeper communion than could be got in day-to-day talk with colleagues and friends.

Once my daughter was settled in nursery, I drove out beyond the bounds of town to the region's hospice to explain and offer myself: they had a befriending programme where volunteers were trained to give an hour of respite to those caring for terminally ill family members, but might they consider me for a role of my own creation? To let me be alongside any patients pained by regret, as I had been? An encounter different in kind to the slow and steady talking cure of counselling; a discomfort not touched by opiates from the palliative care team; what perhaps the chaplains there did for those who were still comfortable with people of faith? Me as a lay version of that? A person able to simply sit and listen to difficult things that could not be fixed. There to help the dying preserve in words moments of joy that were strong in mind as they got ready to go?

They might not have said yes to such an unusual request, but when I went along the corridor with my interviewer to hand in my application, another strangely timed encounter happened – as with the arrival of my grandmother's inheritance.

The woman in charge of personnel paperwork looked at my name and seemed to recognise it.

'I worked at the university for years, and never met you there, but you were held in high regard by my division. Are you joining us next?' Said smiling, with her hand held out to shake mine.

This simple exchange through a doorway was character reference enough, even before the formal ones were called and checked. All my years of conscientious office work were not a waste: I'd earned more respect than I'd ever known till then, and now it opened a very different set of rooms.

§

'Trimming and folding paper, thirty years. Machines do it now, but that was my work.' The man across from me mimed the robotic movements he'd performed for so many decades, then shook his head. *Disbelief, amusement, disgust?* I couldn't tell.

It was a Sunday afternoon in a quiet cul-de-sac of a post-war suburb, and he was my first hospice client. In the next few years I would become adept at this: working with the Möbius-strip sensation felt whenever a dying person confided a thing that twisted time and conversation into a strange new shape. I even became bold enough to invite it, saying – just minutes into first meetings – what was true: that we may only have *here and now* together, and so they should speak to me about whatever was most urgent. There was no time for small talk. Instead: *What stories did they not want lost with their life's ending?*

But I was new to it then, and clumsy. A silence happened.

I looked at his photos spread across the polished mahogany table. There were pictures of the home itself being built, and I saw the beautiful achievement of it for a boy born poor during wartime, whose education ended with evacuation.

'What did you spend your pay packet on, once the bills were paid?'

Idiot. The kind of question an oral historian asks, not one soul to another when death is near. But it animated him at last, this family man of few words who was being prompted by his loving wife, so we'd made more of a list than a life story: *his James 125 motorbike, their green Morris Austin, dancing at the Streatham Locarno.*

Now, like a music box wound and opened, he spoke for long, lyrical minutes of a single night beside an Italian lake in the late 1960s: their first foreign holiday, camping. A storm blew up after dark so that the canvas strained and the children cried. He went out into the wind and rain with the mallet to secure the pegs and guy ropes, and found himself in the company of every other man on the site – all of them working together after that to fasten everything that threatened to blow loose and damage the tents, their families.

He died before I got the notes typed up; his wife thanked me for them, and said his anxiety dropped away soon after our recording.

It was such a slight and uncertain service I had set out to render, *but neither was it nothing*, I told myself whenever a new address and name came through.

I was giving away my time to strangers, but in return how much depth and dimension it gave to my days in those years before my son and daughter began school. That otherwise frantic life stage, in which I was working part-time in a job I'd now outgrown just to keep a safety net of paid childminders in place.

My condition of total openness to whoever asked for me

was transformative. A new measure for life and how to live it: my worth judged not by salary, or targets, or competition, but the quality of attention I could make available to another human. Could I sit for an hour or more and put everything else aside? Attend fully to each new person's voice, their gestures, and the things they kept around them?

Yes. And once I'd assured them of my motives for being there, they wanted to speak, very much, so that we entered together into still waters running deep.

I did, early on, have an ambitious idea – project manager that I still was – of creating a national listening service that could tend to every hospice and care home so that no soul should go to their death unheard and unburdened (just as I'd trained a team of student ambassadors at the university to travel into inner-city areas). Still that wish to make order, to tidy life, its emotions. But the stories I heard resisted me. They were moving and mysterious, like their tellers. Irreducible.

The man who dismissed my question about family photos on the wall. That was his late wife of many years . . . but he wanted to talk about a woman who had just died. *This one, look.* He only had a year with her. And before *that* he'd seen her just once, in his twenties – at her engagement to his best friend. Love at first sight. Good thing they emigrated soon after, he supposed. The friend sent photos sometimes. Life went on, as it does. Marriage. Work. Children. Then she wrote a few years back to say she was widowed and returning to England, knowing no one. Would he meet her off the plane? He did . . . and she walked straight into his arms! And then all they got was this one year before she died and he began to . . .

Much-travelled woman who'd been a beauty. It made life so easy – doors opened, men took care of her, paid for every-thing. She danced, had parties. Yes, there was always money, fun. She didn't see it coming. Old age. *The invisibility.* She'd been so *angry* all these years and still was. And her children were in the next room crying. Wanting her to tell them how much she loved them. But she wouldn't, and I couldn't make her. She had only ever wanted to travel, and did. That's how it was back then, in her set. Put them in school and go abroad. It was her granddaughters she wanted to leave a message for. To tell them to *refuse it*. Babies, children. It wasn't what mattered to her . . .

The schoolteacher who was loved, admired. Had no regrets really, only sadness at this illness of course. And yet, funny to find himself thinking about a lad he was at school with who went into the priesthood. His own family had always been churchgoers but it was done with a light touch. Social as much as anything. Community. So he was embarrassed, perhaps, to show how serious it was for him? Yes. Nothing tragic. But odd to find that boy on his mind so often. To feel a bit of envy disturbing his conscience as he got ready to go.

Last Offices

WHAT GOLDEN DAYS NYE AND I, once so isolated, were sharing in those years with other mothers and their husbands, our lives so intertwined that the collected children could run about at weekend barbecues and camping trips finding cuddles and comfort from any of us. And we discussed such intimate things: our bodies, ageing parents, work hopes, money worries. Our friendships as fires lit against those bleak first months of new parenthood that we all of us shuddered to remember.

But I was compelled now to keep travelling out beyond the edge of town to where people our age and younger were dying: strapping middle-aged men – football players, cricketers – who'd been diagnosed with wasting conditions that take body and breath before the mind; mothers who'd be leaving behind children the age of ours.

No one asked me what I was doing there, or why: a gap in understanding had opened up around this part of my life, and I was beginning to feel myself at a new distance from my identity as a parent.

Because wasn't our talk turning more and more to house prices and the school choices that were fast coming up, instead of how to raise our children outside the orthodoxies of our time and place (what had bonded us all to begin with)? How had the charmed days of our first communal seasons – that clearing we women made for ourselves, impenetrable to our men – given way so soon to the outside world? All of its expensive, unrelenting standards crowding back in.

When did we start paying for everything? For our toddlers to walk on beams, roll on mats? To swim short laps with precise technique? To kick balls and hit them? And so many fees of our own: homeopathy, yoga, spinning, strength-training. Equipment for all this: mats, monitors. Shoes engineered to feel as though our bare soles met the ground when running.

Surrounded by those good people and everyday comforts, I couldn't seem to get the same nourishment from it I once had. I began to suspect then that I'd never recover from having been stripped so fast of my health and false sense of security.

And nor did I want to.

§

So what should I do with my second life, really, once the children were both in school?

The university had been my mother ship and anchor since I arrived there at nineteen, and soon I would be forty. The way a childhood home remains important for adults from loving families, so workplaces can be for those without that. Campus was my heartland: I knew all the jackdaw nests and trees claimed by magpies; was on close terms with its porters, cleaners and cooks. What my first teacher had promised me, it was: a sort of modern-day monastery where the seasons repeated and young administrators grew into its grey-haired keepers of institutional order.

But I was no longer very central to its running. I'd let a little more seniority go each year, sand from my pockets, in return for time with my children so that – in the months before my daughter started school – my projects had become piecemeal, a make-work. Too, team changes meant there was no place for me any more in the building that had been home from home since my twenties.

Of all the hundreds of offices across that large campus, the one they gave me was a huge corner room of my own in the corridor where I'd attended all my English tutorials as a young undergraduate dreaming of the artist's life. I found its privacy and possibility painful – uncomfortable reminder of what I might have been – but made a joke of it when sending the address to Yuri:

FORGOTTEN OFFICE,
ON THE STAIRWELL,
ABOVE THE MUSIC PRACTICE ROOMS,
BETWEEN ARTS A & B

Apart from my daughter, who used to play under the desk and spin on my chair after her mornings at nursery, he was my only real visitor in the nine months I had it. It caught his imagination, I think, and he began calling on me each month for the first time in four years. We continued chaste, but he started to touch my arm, my back, as we walked. To confide more deeply about his work and health worries. To pick me flowers and say their names – *bird's-foot trefoil, wood anemone*. A fatherly gesture that would have had me giddy with gladness when we first became close; now, as a mother, I knew as much as he did, from having knelt, field guide in hand, to learn for my children parts of the natural world I didn't already know.

He was still overpaying on his pension, and working long hours instead of trusting others to share the load – rehearsing, as ever, ways he might negotiate a *golden handcuffs* deal to leave. Only man other than Nye for whom I'd ever felt affection, I listened to all this, although I no longer shared his cramped ideas of how a life could be.

Give me your arm, old toad; Help me down Cemetery Road: lines from Philip Larkin, who'd conducted a minor-key life as head librarian at a northern university – words that were part of my and Yuri's shared sensibility, both of us blinkered to risk by our disrupted upbringings. What one of us would say whenever we explored whatever churchyard was near the pub we'd eaten at.

But now I sat with those who really were about to go into the ground; I had come close to it myself. Unlived lives were no longer a whimsy to me, but a matter of awful, urgent sorrow. I was still only shuttling between home, school, hospice and this forgotten office, but my soul had begun calling me to come outside while there was still time.

Child's Play

WATCH ME WHILE I SLEEP, MUMMY.

What my son asked for at three for what felt like a month of Sundays, opening his eyes again and again to check I was still there, gazing at his face. And his cry on waking always: *Daddy, Mummy, where are you? Come and get me. I'm back! I'm back!*

AWAKE, SLEEPING BEAUTY.

His sister's insistent morning ritual at the same age. How her brother and I knelt by her bed at the start of each day, exclaiming over this extraordinary girl we'd found, so that her stout little body, listening, wriggled with pleasure before she began her pantomime of waking to the day.

Seven years of tending very small children in that way had now just ended. And on the day my daughter finally started school, I was invited to several homes across town by the good women with whom I'd passed that endless-seeming time of parks and rainy days at kitchen tables.

I loved them, but my eyes were fixed that morning on the far-off fields. An instinct telling me I must begin now and not stop on what had been unsettling me since the near-death. To find a way to reach fully for something beyond town, home, family. I watched my friends go away in different directions then simply walked towards the horizon line.

At the top of the hill beyond the school, I came upon a huge hawthorn tree, low to the ground and creaking, hung about with fleece that fluttered like torn Tibetan prayer flags. I got on all fours, crawling under spiked branches towards the hollow of its old exposed roots, and there I stayed all that first day my girl was away from me. Each time children ran out for play down below, I was certain, despite the distance, of her voice in the yard.

It became my deliberate routine for the rest of that week I'd taken off work: sitting vigil in sight of the school, so as to suffer and celebrate the separation of her and me.

How had we been together?

It was urgent to me, before starting out on the next stage of their lives and mine, to re-examine all the thousands of ordinary hours I'd spent with my son and daughter: who we were when there was no one there to know or care how I treated them.

Watch me while I sleep, Mummy.
Awake, Sleeping Beauty.

The cat's mother: what I'd have said if anyone before then had asked what kind of caregiver I'd been. In childhood, I'd seen the strays that scavenged from nearby farms become fastidious teachers once they had a litter. Tender, patient. I had cared for my son and daughter that way, but because I kept a little internal distance always – resisting the physical passion other women described for their children – I felt myself a different, lesser breed of mother.

But there was another story of those years. One of compassion and conscientiousness. Of fun and fantasy. Performed for no pay, no status, only the delight of that small boy and girl.

So many games I improvised to meet their need for hours of play and close attention when I was too disabled by back pain to move very much.

Catching the Moon. Torch beam that I bounced around a darkened room in the last excruciating hour before their father came home each evening – letting it linger on a spot until they grabbed at it, only to send the light skipping off and away from them once again.

Mechanical Dancer. Me as an old rusted doll they'd found, who had to be dusted and oiled before they could wind me up – and then I'd begin, slowly, very slowly, to move just a little . . . a finger, then a toe – and then my eyes opened and I rose to my feet, turning about like the ballerina in a jewellery box. Pointed toes, pirouettes – until my spring was unwound and I lay myself back down.

These and other amusements, all played out behind our big bay windows that I kept curtainless, even after dusk in winter, so anyone outside could look in. Not exhibitionism but a safety mechanism. The terrible things in my childhood took place in private, behind thick net curtains. *What if such fury came one day roaring out through my mouth and hands when Nye was not home to rescue our children?* Being always on show in rooms illuminated and open to view like a doll's house – this, I felt, would keep me in check, and them protected.

By putting on a constant and exhausting show, I'd kept them both safe. But those little rituals that they each asked for, again and again, with such fervency: what were those?

Watch me while I sleep, Mummy.
Awake, Sleeping Beauty.

At this new distance from my girl and boy, I understood of a sudden what was missing in my own development: children who are safe know exactly what they need, and are unafraid to ask for it. Again and again. Their desires are not always being sandbagged or buried or rationed.

What might be obvious to others had for me, there and then, the force of revelation. I came back off the hillside at the end of that week with it ringing inside me, as if I were a bell being sounded.

How would it be to give to myself, for even a short while, such kindness? To spend time learning or recovering what I loved, what I yearned for? To ask for exactly what I needed, as my children were able to do? I'd been so concerned in my first life on becoming safe and secure, and intent since the birth and its aftermath on giving care – to the children, other mothers, hospice patients.

Could I do it? Learn how to play, and not for others' sakes, but my own?

§

'I don't think I can go back to work.'

Words I never imagined saying. I got my first Saturday job at twelve, and worked six days a week through every summer holiday from the age of fourteen in cafés and seaside hotels. The year I took off between college and university, I did double shifts at a countryside resort for weeks at a time, in return for bed, meals and minimum wage. The day I handed in my dissertation at one end of the university's admin building, I'd started an internship in an office just down the corridor. And aside from my brief season in London working in television, I'd stayed on campus ever since.

Only ever able to imagine scarcity, I'd never considered a time before retirement when I might be without paid employment, but there I was telling hard-working Nye that I needed to stop. Now. And not even to retrain or apply for something else. To do what, then?

To sink. Or swim.

Instead of the anger I anticipated, he made a noise that was either relief or frustration. Which?

Both. *Thank God*, he said. *You've got there. I thought you'd never let go of the university. It has kept you on such a tight leash, and me with it.*

I said next everything I was frightened by and ashamed to

ask: to rely on his salary when I knew what it was like to be a mother and child left on short rations by a man; to seem like a dropout to friends and family; to ask him to keep working while I stopped . . . *how selfish it was.*

I went mute then, biting my nails, and Nye touched me on the chin to have me look up, and be an adult not a child. To own what I'd asked for.

'Why can't this time ahead be a balancing of the books between us, Tan? Wasn't there a cost to you, your health, to have our son and daughter? You're in so much pain, and so tired. But I can't decide this for you.'

We did the sums next – shared prudence with money we'd had from the start – finding that with the ruinous nursery fees gone, and if we stuck to strict economies with food, I could now – barring any further accidents and emergencies – *buy time.* Be fully free for a few years to swim out into my days, if I could find the courage to let go of the side.

To Be a Bold Swimmer

IN MY FIRST MONTHS BEYOND THE OFFICE, I only hibernated.

Overwhelmed by so much unstructured time, I shuffled around the too-quiet house doing odd, invalid stuff that in no way justified letting go of a monthly pay cheque and pension: plucking at the guitar I'd always planned to learn; reading classic children's books I was without growing up. Trying to write in a tiny palm-sized reporter's pad, and finding it like engraving onto glass – any way with words I'd had in my twenties long gone. A relief when the clock reached three each day and I could fetch the children back with the purpose they provided.

Perhaps it was that, combined with the first hot day, that had me – for the first time – react against being with a hospice patient.

It was my third visit to an overheated house in an outlying village where I sat with an elderly client who wanted only to sift through photos. Not even ones of her family beyond the door, but images instead of distant Victorian dead. My place to sit bored and almost ignored while she wrote careful genealogical notes about vanished rich industrialists. There was something painful to me about that choice, and the way the woman's frail hands clung to those old branches on a family tree, needing to turn leaves in a fragile album as her last days fell away. It brought my mournful early years with Mother back to mind, too: that bloody black box I'd been made to study containing relics of my great-grandmother's small dead daughter.

Even when I was back outside – car windows down, hair blowing, driving too fast along the sun-baked summer lanes – I couldn't shift the smell of old crypts. I wanted to be *washed clean*. Of that morning's visit, but also my own inwards-turning habits. My office years were ended, but I was still keeping myself confined in the working week – a prison-yard mindset.

The coast was close by, but the tame English Channel had only ever made me homesick for the real sea of my childhood's North Devon and Cornish beaches: those jagged black cliffs and fast Atlantic waves that tumbled me into a flotsam, a jetsam; happy, self-forgetful, carefree. When I moved away at sixteen, I turned my back to the ocean, restricting myself to fields. Now, though, my want for cold water was urgent. I needed to strip off, plunge in. Exorcise those corseted, crinolined women. Recover a body I'd been removed from for far too long.

There was an outdoor pool at the bottom of my adopted home town, open every summer since Queen Victoria's reign: spring-fed, unheated, hidden behind a tall brick-and-flint wall – a source of joy for generations. But I'd only ever sat on the grass while my toddlers paddled, feeling too ashamed of my baby weight to go in the water.

Now I scrabbled through my cupboards for a costume, only to find an old one with slack elastic, faded and grey like a dogfish skin washed in on the tide.

Mortifying to go through the gate once it opened, and head to the changing rooms, and peel off my jeans, and confront the knicker marks at my waist, my hips. Worse still to walk then to the deep end in my loose suit and be seen by anyone who looked. I'd come to wash off the horror got from photos of old widows, but now I wished this was still the way we women dressed. Covered, compressed.

I got in, propelled by a wish to hide underwater. Each length of front crawl – only stroke I could do – had me face down in such piercing cold that my eardrums rang with it. And to go a hundred and fifty feet, wall to wall, left me clinging to the side, gasping, while pretending to admire the pine trees and clouds overhead.

Fool. Fool. Fool. Breathe. *Fool. Fool. Fool.*

But when I got out after twelve lung-straining laps and sat with my bare legs stuck out to catch the sun?

Joy.

And once I'd gone shivering to the kiosk to buy hot chocolate in a polystyrene cup, a big kid's smile spreading across my face just as when my cold hands clutched a warm drink on my childhood beach?

Joy.

How strange to have forgotten so long. How simple it could be, to let the body lead.

§

There was a fairy tale I read often with my daughter at this time. THE PRINCESS AND THE FROG. In it, the girl is by the water's edge and happy to play alone, throwing her golden ball up into the air, again and again.

While drying after my now-daily lengths of the outdoor pool in that first out-of-work summer, I dared to recall my own happiest times, finding that I could write of them after swimming with a fluency I'd lacked back in the house: the laps releasing sense memories and giving me a rhythm for lines in my notebook.

What energy I used to have at seven, eight, nine. What drive. How, in the sea – away from the thick nicotine misery of home – I threw myself against the waves like a freedom fighter, my heavy wooden surfboard held up as battering ram, believing myself invincible.

I'd been vain on the beach, too, instead of self-effacing.

Yes, how I'd loved my body back then, back there, so briefly. Its strength. Its beauty: the down on my legs which went gold in the sun; a deep white V on each foot from my flip-flops. Even injuries pleased me, so that I counted them like coins, my treasure. Status symbols. Among all the people on the beach I believed myself the most brown, most bruised.

Since then, it had only ever been in lovemaking that my body had come alive. But now, there at the outdoor pool and despite my calloused feet and varicose veins, I felt newly alert to my nerve endings.

Youth is wasted on the young. One of my mother-in-law's many sayings.

Let me not waste any more of this second life still so new, then.

I got back in and swam more laps.

§

So began my most intoxicating summer since the one, twenty years earlier, in which Nye and I had met.

It wasn't being in the water that thrilled me so much as the delicious after-swim rituals. Because it was there on hot paving slabs beyond the deep end that I got to lie beside other adults naked, like me, of their domestic selves, their work ones. We spread ourselves out like seals, unselfconscious, turning front to back, side to side, towards the sun or shade. Few words were ever exchanged – nothing beyond asking about the books by our towels or sharing tips on stroke techniques – but there was a feeling of fellowship, frank and physical. Just sometimes a little passing comment would hint at a loss that had led to new perspective, and we'd nod in recognition. *Enough said.* We were the ones who'd had our wake-up calls, and answered them by freeing up hours or even days.

It was also a late love affair with self that began in that summer of my fortieth year. At the very age when women start to fear being invisible, this is when I got my late bloom of confidence.

How beautiful I felt in my big brown jumper knitted during the baby years, designed with two deep pockets to hold dummies, snacks, small toys; now I pulled it on over my wet costume before tying a bright headscarf over my hair (as Granny and other West Country women had; what I decided on, very young, as a special emblem of female grace). The things I had around me became charged too, and talismanic, from being just for me at last: Thermos flask; red tin mug, blue-handled pocketknife to peel my apples; musty army-surplus rucksack kept packed with poetry for this blissful time alone. In the water, I was vivid, kinetic, all flashes of brown skin and strong arms; afterwards I felt myself a still life, composed and contemplative.

Yes, I was in love with myself, there by the water, but not like Narcissus, unheeding of others. Instead, feeling so at home in my body freed my attention to turn outwards, fully and forever. We are taught so often that love of self is shameful and should be curbed, but I believe now insecurity makes in us a distracting background noise that drowns out the precious here and now. My mind had never been so clear and open as in those outdoor days. I read with even more hunger than before, devouring Buddhism, existential philosophers, old Chinese poets. Had time for lonely people on park benches who found me a friendly face. And the small notebook I'd struggled to fill in the early months at home: it was followed by ten, twenty, thirty, more – all of them running rich with what was around me.

How I began to spend my time that season would enlarge my life in a way I would only understand later, looking back. At the water's edge that very first day when I stepped out from the hidden and habitual along with my clothes, I couldn't know that even a middle-aged mother swimming laps in a small town can send ripples through the universe. But it did.

Outsider

The pure, extravagant, yearning, questioning artist's face

Mayfly

HAVING ONCE COME SO FAST and close to death, I had apprenticed myself that first spring and summer to the slow and steady pursuit of awareness. Laps of the outdoor pool from May to September; pens, paper; people passing by my park bench; birds I fed with bread from my pockets; ancient poets who wrote about patience: those were my first teachers.

But then the days began to shorten and the air to turn cold. The other swimmers and sunbathers with whom I'd spent so much time returned to their offices and private homes. I was the last person in the pool before it closed for the season, floating face skyward with arms outstretched as leaves from the crack willow tree beyond the wall landed around me; myself likewise surplus to requirements.

Soon after, I received an offer for full-time project work back on campus from the new year, throwing me a line back into my old amniotic fluid of routine and financial security. It should have been a source of unambiguous relief, allowing me to enjoy a few more months of freedom before returning, refreshed, to normal adult life.

Instead, I was cast into confusion, so that I sat crying one day beside a chaplain at the hospice.

'Look at Blake. Samuel Palmer. George Herbert. Read Merton. You belong to a fine tradition.' What she, an Ignatian, said to me, atheist, when I wept to be dreaming always of God, of churches. That beckoning light which poured forth, night after night, from those buildings I was free to enter, and would not.

(*My place is outside*. What I continued to say each time before waking to the same slow tears that were falling into tissues the older, listening woman kept handing me.)

I asked her, sobbing, about *callings* – how she, a religious person, understood them.

'Because it feels, to me,' I said, 'like a mistake in my brain. I just want to enjoy my family and the women friends I've made so late. Go back to work and feel grateful for it. Why won't it go away and leave me alone, this yearning for deeper connection?'

She smiled and said I was wanting my *sealed orders* – for my purpose to be revealed and myself relieved of uncertainty, but it didn't work like that. Vocations, *particularly the spiritual ones*, required of us first *discernment*. We must learn to filter and distil our soul's small voice before it could become a trustworthy compass.

She walked me then to my car, helping to carry the un-familiar texts about faith I had borrowed from her shelves.

'Listen to your dream. Stay outside a bit longer. See what comes.'

What she said before I drove back to town. The books I wouldn't open for a long while, but her parting words became a ration of courage that helped me decide against a return to work.

§

My outsider years. What I call them now, the seasons that fol-lowed, and which are preserved in half a million handwritten words in tiny diaries that fit, like honeycomb, in a box beneath my bed.

So much rich experience that has little or no currency in how our worth is usually measured in the modern world. A heron's wing that brushed my cheek while I sat long and still in deep shade by a river; a fox with a rabbit in her mouth who ran into me on a quiet woodland path; a moment when the blossom came down from every cherry tree along a residential street so I felt married to the day.

And so it is a tender thing, admitting to a purpose so at odds with the values of my time and place. How, after decades of saving, I became profligate. Giving myself *out* and *away*, so that while I continued to practise patience in one sense – sitting alone in the flower gardens, doing my thirty laps a day or more – I was burning with a mayfly fervour to meet and merge with other people.

In my second summer by the pool, I began writing a story called THE CURE FOR SLEEP in which a woman, after near-death, returns (medical mystery) without the need to rest. Who creates chaos by lavishing love and care on strangers, ceaselessly, for weeks, until she dies, suddenly, desiccated, insect-obscure on the far edge of a busy city scene. Modern version of the swallow in Wilde's THE HAPPY PRINCE, that little bird which does itself to death delivering alms to the townsfolk. This woman like that: a mechanism of excess generosity.

What I might have chosen in real life if a simple nip and tuck in my brain could have delivered me one ever-present year: awake without strain day and night until I reached event horizon – that place promising an eternal communion of souls that I'd turned back from in the ambulance.

Shy as I'd always been, I wanted to begin living a *public* life, not a private one. *To make something happen*, for the good of myself and others. However slight, however brief.

As ants wait for a precise set of conditions to combine before they can take wing and mate in a single night each year, so I was restless and ready for change. *Chance favours the prepared mind* – saying of a famous scientist I hoped might prove true for me too, if I stayed outside and kept putting myself in the way of whatever came.

Yes, how hard this is, more than writing of my childhood, my body, my marriage: to say what I was doing in that brief midlife season. It sounds so naïve, so naked, to say I was *unfolding into the full reach of my privilege and protection in law*, like an insect warming its wings: walking outdoors, talking to men in public places, revelling in reading and eating alone in restaurants. To live to the limits of what was allowed – while preparing to venture further still perhaps.

As I walked around in my newly free days, I couldn't stop thinking about all the women through history who had been denied ease and opportunity. And even though I lived in a time and place relatively free of oppression, how many of us shrank from being judged, mocked, misunderstood? Mother had lived in fear of this and Nye's mother was sceptical of anything that spoke of ambition and individuality. And most of the brilliant friends I'd made since becoming a parent spoke of feeling never fully equipped or equal to what they were doing.

Imposter syndrome: We can none of us afford such a haemorrhage of energy: what I wanted to say to women who sat at café tables talking about maternal guilt and to-do lists.

I might never, I knew, find myself in a time of war or injustice when what I did – on a bus, in the street, or with words on paper – carried great danger or consequence. My life might always be small, personal and without hardship, but it seemed to me a moral imperative not to waste any more such safety. I wanted to revel in nature, sunlight. Take risks. Find ways to demonstrate my freedom, and encourage it in others.

Pavement Art

TO BE A PERSON WHO HAS CROSSED OVER from fantasy to action, someone whose dreams and desires have been released into the wild instead of being locked inside them always, unshared. This is what I wanted for myself, acutely, by the spring of my second year beyond the university, so that I roamed the bounds of town at dawn and dusk like a zoo animal looking through the glass for its own kind. But when it did happen for me at last – that first small step into a public life – it came in a way I could never have imagined.

It was the first bank holiday in May, and a protected eighty-year-old chestnut tree in the community field across from our home had been skinned of its bark by vandals overnight.

As when horses get attacked while out in their pastures: how it was. Obscene-looking, against nature, of alien intent: a flaying that was deep and neat and deliberate. *A nightmare.* What those of us who gathered there kept saying, as if we might wake next day to find it intact again, unharmed.

Nye and the field's other stewards phoned for experts, wondering if it could be bandaged in some saving way: adult impulse to right a wrong. My own reaction was slower taking shape and came from a primitive place not tapped before. It was, I understood that evening, sitting at my desk that looked out on the tree, the first time I could not metabolise a shock by reading. Words would not salve this. A physical response was needed, but what? An answer came immediately I asked, with odd but compelling logic.

The railings that ran the length of the field – intricate, gone brown and brittle – I would paint them. By myself, for as long as it took. A quiet defiance. The tree was beyond repair but I could lavish care on the space around it.

I began the next day and, as with my first laps of the pool a year before, it released something in me as soon as I started. A sense of place last felt as a girl when whole days were spent in that tempo – down low, slow – at whatever I'd been induced to do: picking gooseberries, podding peas, crawling after a tractor for potatoes pulled up by its spinner. Physical rhythms of a rural childhood that my body had been missing ever since. And the sensory denseness of that time – the sweet powdered milk for calves we children swallowed by the handful until we choked and foamed at the mouth; our heady-smelling creosoted sheds where we felt each other up – this had something of that too. Everything coming to me neat between the railings I knelt at: a magpie rattling from the urine-tinged hawthorn; arguments of couples coming home, beery from barbecues; the ice cream van's jewellery-box version of *Greensleeves*.

I went to bed that first night emptied of self, saturated with day. *On to something.*

Just to sand and prime such a very long run of railings was the work of months, and after keeping it up, and to regular hours, I had become, in my headscarf and paint-stained apron, an accidental performance artist. Alone in the street at my stubborn task – outside my usual bubbles of family and friends – I attracted all-comers: window cleaners, delivery drivers, parking wardens, pensioners who trundled by with their shopping trolleys. And so I decided to make a game from it: to speak only when spoken to, and not at all if gestures would do.

Like the Forth Bridge, eh? Smile, nod, keep painting.

Community service, is it? Smile, nod, keep painting.

Getting paid? Smile, shake head, keep painting.

How many left now? Smile, shrug, keep painting.

A few people, very few, stopped to look without speaking. I painted then with elaborate care, my brush running intimately over the braided metal poles. Erotic, unexpectedly so, to be knelt, neck bent, and watched at work. Yes, it was the geisha fantasy I'd had as a girl – something I'd enjoyed only rarely as an adult, mainly in talk with Yuri. The charge got when my skill was admired, so that I shivered with what I called a *stringed-instrument sensation*. A humming of pleasure and purpose.

It was playful like that. Silly, sensuous.

Only towards the end, a whole season in, did it deepen into something more serious. A retired neighbour in ill health came out carefully with a cup of tea for me, and then stayed there waiting until I pulled my earphones out.

'Why have you kept going? And why alone?'

I took off my sunglasses.

There it was: the question that required an answer.

'Because after years of only reading, I find I can write in the evenings with an ease in proportion to the hours my hand has painted in the day. And I almost died after the birth of my first child, as you know, and I have been less troubled in sleep by *that* since I began working at *this*.' I took a breath. 'And . . . I was not born here, but *belong* now, through effort.'

It was my private voice, and authorial. The one I'd hidden in notebooks till then – earnest as a book gone out of fashion.

He took me by the hands, sticky with paint though they were, and we stood there a while, not speaking.

What a strange portrait we must have made: two out-of-work people, bent-backed and a bit frail, in that street like other streets in our expensive part of town, so quiet during the week.

Lost and Found

I'D CARRIED ON DAYDREAMING of the writer's life ever since my degree years, yet I never wrote anything beyond my diaries and so had no real hope of ever being published.

But the season I spent painting the railings moved me to story at last: seeing a local psychogeography project advertised back on campus, I made myself show up for the briefing – me, who'd never attended a single social activity as an undergraduate. I listened, heart going hard, as each person was asked to share an idea and my own turn came closer. Said then, speaking timidly and too fast, that I might describe a vandalised tree in my street and my strong response to it?

Once home, I went straight upstairs and began to type, finishing within an hour, and finding my essay only one word short of the length limit. I read it aloud to the cats on the bedspread, then sent it away.

It would be accepted.

I was certain of this, a belief that never faltered in the months it took for the deadline to pass and the editors to reply.

How was I so sure?

From a new density in my bones; an unfamiliar sense of being at the very centre of my life in the moment of writing. What I'd made was short, and local, but it was also *concentrated*: a story of pure experience.

I was invited to read it in a campus lecture theatre that autumn, and on my birthday, of all dates, so that I had a rare chance to be reborn as a bolder and braver incarnation in the very place where I'd been a reclusive student and shy administrator.

Through all the years I'd studied and worked at the university, the occasional need to give presentations was only ever something to suffer: the nerves had never gone away despite all the extra training I sought. But now I found in myself a fierce wish to speak so that I was impatient to begin, while also mourning the evening's end already: *Oh what if I never got to do it again?*

There was, though, a shadow side to this bright moment, my late metamorphosis. I was without fear, yes, but also missing the person I wanted most to read for – the only one who would understand how much I'd changed.

§

Once I'd left office life fully, Yuri began to call on me at my new and bigger house. Not as often, due to ever-increasing pressures in his own workplace but still to a regular pattern: our old monthly routine become instead seasonal. He astonished me in the first summer by saying he'd join me at the pool, and it was touching to see him stripped of his shirt and tie, holding his head clear of the water in an awkward breaststroke, while I – with a fast front crawl – was already at the far end waiting.

Then came autumn, and he arrived full of deep emotion I couldn't, for once, fathom; I suggested we abandon the lunch I'd made and walk under the walnut trees just across the road – having an instinct that he needed to speak without being seen. While we used my long blue skirt to collect all the nuts not ruined by squirrels, he began to talk of a friend from long ago who had just died. The family had contacted him, Yuri, with details of the service . . . *and he hadn't even replied.* This and other regrets about his life and how he lived it. *Money. Work.* We arrived back at his parked car and I said something that had just occurred to me, horribly. *If you died fast like that, no one in your office would know I'd been your friend. I wouldn't be told.* It was a statement, not a question. I guessed – of a sudden, like a fruit fallen hard from a tree – what had never been discussed between us: that while Nye knew about Yuri, and was interested to hear what we talked about always, in Yuri's home life all these years – private as he was, and living so far away from his workplace – *I may not exist.* Tears happened in my eyes, and before I could turn away to hide them, he stepped forward to kiss me on the forehead – lightly, precisely, as I'd seen Nye do to our daughter sometimes when she moved him to it.

After this rush of feeling from him, no word until the next spring, when he needed me at no notice for the first time. *Could someone mind the children so I could meet him in a park we both liked?*

I arrived there before him and stood in light rain under cherry blossom, realising that I was in *the prime of life* finally. Fine white shirt with a loose bow. Tiger-eye beads warm at my throat. Old blue raincoat belted tight at the waist and torn at the shoulder like the song. Green headscarf covering my still-bright hair. And the afternoon was perfected, also: cattle were grazing nearby, gorgeous brown milk cows; the trees were heavy with pink flowers, and the sky turning that colour too. But when Yuri arrived, I saw he was blind to it – me, the day. *His job: it was ending.* And so I listened, as I always had, until he'd turned his shock into a form of words he could use with others who'd need to be told.

'This is the last time I'll see you.'

What I said on parting. His house was somewhere on the far side of London; there'd soon be no reason for him to travel down here again.

He took both my hands. *No, no. I was important to him. This was his chance to start doing things differently, to have me meet his family, as he'd met mine . . .*

A feature of our measured friendship was how rarely we had ever sent messages each to each, and only then short ones to agree on our next lunch or walk. We were never chatty between times. It was an odd arrangement but one I trusted, and cherished, it never having let me down: in ten years, Yuri didn't once cancel or forget. So when his leaving date came around with no word from him, I sent an email to his work address – the only contact of his I'd ever had. And received back?

An auto-reply.

He was gone, and lost to me.

The boarding-school boy who'd been moved from country to country at no notice, keeping his thoughts to himself and his few small treasures in a little tin box beneath his pillow – whatever I'd been to the man he'd become was likewise put to sleep now, and he'd never – I knew – reawaken it.

My name being said. Time to rise and go on stage.

I walked to the front and spoke without waver. Aware, with each word not heard by Yuri, that I was moving beyond the old and aching legacy of every school nativity and prize-giving, when I'd look for Father and find him never there.

Beyond the Pale

THOSE DREAMS THAT LAST ONLY LONG ENOUGH for the saving of a soul: how we were arranged in the waking day of that early new year, me and the man who had rung the bell. I held my door frame so I wouldn't faint or float.

'This is the *real thing*.'

The person on my doorstep was holding my essay about the tree and the railings. (I'd put copies of it into the community field's Christmas mailing, just to enjoy the idea it might be read by even a few of the several hundred people in town who supported our small charity.)

'How have you conveyed so much in so few words? I counted them!' The man tapped the paper, showing all his pencil marks.

Aware of this being a fairy-tale rare exchange, I kept quiet instead of being self-deprecating and going deaf to his praise. Felt the day tilt on its axis – life was changing shape, there and then.

My words were in the hands of an artist whose work I'd admired long before our first and only chance meeting just a month earlier. Shown in the Tate, the Guggenheim, his sculptures were as important to me as those by Barbara Hepworth, Henry Moore. His ideas about life, like theirs, took up space and touched others, as mine did not.

But now here he was, saying how moved he was by what *I'd* made.

§

When our paths had first crossed at the end of December, he was only a person on the pavement below my writing desk, standing beside a stout man with a clipboard. The two huge lime trees they were looking at belonged to the bungalow across the way that had just been sold, but they mattered to me as if they were my own. Growing so close together, they were heart-shaped in summer, bronchial in winter. My first sight each morning and last at night.

I knew I should not go out there. It was not, of course, my business. And this would be no good way to meet a new neighbour, if this is what the older man might be. But I'd been sitting stricken over a blank page the whole morning, and the bin in the kitchen needed to go out, so down I went.

'Please just tell me. Are you the bungalow's new owner, and planning to have the trees removed? It's just that I look out on them from my desk up there, and if they're going to go, I'd rather know than be worried and wondering.' My face burned. *Stupid rude fool.*

'We're almost finished. I'll come back later and tell you what I'm doing.' His gracious response, said with a wry smile, only made my colour rise harder, faster.

Back inside, I put my forehead against the hallway wall and before I could think of what to do next with my failing day, the bell rang.

He was back. He liked, he said, that I cared about the trees. He worked with wood, so he wanted to keep them standing. Although – *as I could see!* – they'd grown huge and needed care. I nodded too much, said sorry several times.

'Are you an artist?' I'd already begun to close the door, but he was looking now at my apron.

'This? Oh no. I wore it when I painted the railings over there, look. I'm trying to become a writer, actually, but the only things I've had published are short and local. And so late! I do feel a fool to be beginning at my age.' I apologised again, this time for talking too much.

He began to go away then, but I called him back, remembering at last my manners.

We shook hands.

I said my name.

He said his.

Heaviness filled my belly. *The embarrassment.*

'So when you said you worked in wood you meant you were a sculptor of it. I have a big book about you in the next room . . .'

He was surprised I knew his art, and I told him how I'd come across it by chance a decade ago, wandering into an exhibition during my first summer as a mother. Objects unlike any I'd seen before – skewed ladders, giant tables, cracked balls and boxes – which felt true of how my own substance and structure had been warped by childbirth, its aftermath. It was, I said, the same shock I'd got on my first contact with art at fifteen, bussed up to London for a day. We'd been taken there to see the Hockney swimming pools, but it was a room full of huge misshapen figures – tiny heads, vast backs – that had me fall away from friends and stand quiet. A giddy, initiate sensation, as if someone wise had come up close to whisper in my ear: *See this. Know it. You can make things that are like nothing else, and people will travel, will pay, to be near it.*

We smiled at that and shook hands on our strange meeting. I shut the door. It was, for a few days afterwards, a story I told at my own expense for the amusement of Nye and a few others in my circle who knew who he was. Then I thought no more of it.

§

Now, with the door closed on my second meeting with the sculptor, I went to my desk on unsteady legs and wrote what he'd just said on the paper that had resisted me all morning: *You discovered something about the world while painting the fence, and now you must formalise that in your next piece of work.*

What did he mean?

I didn't know, yet I felt a shiver, as at those long-ago exhibitions of his work, and Moore's: a beckoning towards a life played looser, lighter, and by very different rules, if only the right intuitive or even foolhardy leap could be made. Like the idiot in the tarot pack who steps from the cliff into uncertain fortune.

I'd always known how to work hard and go years on scraps of praise. But mightn't I start going further, faster, if I took on a bolder persona for a while?

I looked out at the railings, down at my apron. Called upon my whole stock of story to find a way forward.

There was Twain's Tom Sawyer, who turned his punishment of painting a fence into a spectacle that drew in all his classmates, emptying their pockets of treasure in return for a chance to take over his labour. And Puss in Boots who parlayed an empty sack into a brace of rabbits into a fine suit of clothes and then the king's daughter and a castle for his poor master.

What if I likewise performed my endless diary-writing in public? Unlike my attempts at fiction, I knew I could sustain it, fluent now from years of note-making outside. And I was practised, too, from my hospice work, at speaking with strangers . . .

But how to make it beautiful, alluring?

If I knelt to it, head bowed, headscarved, as I had on the street. And changed the scale, the aesthetics, so my writing conjured other times and places. Having the feel of fairy tale, the proportions of myth.

I made notes. Things to look up. Pillow books. Scheherazade. *One Thousand and One Nights.* Ariadne and the red thread she gives Theseus to navigate the Minotaur's labyrinth. Penelope's loom: how she weaves without cease while hoping for her husband's return.

Imagined then a scroll of paper as long as the pool I'd already spent so many hours beside. Lines of that length, done lap after lap, until I reached some incredible distance.

What patience it would take.

(What nerve.)

To be a woman in middle age, taking up space, claiming attention.

Making an exhibition of myself.

(What Mother said I must never, ever do.)

Beyond the pale.

(Outside the fenced enclosure; into disrepute.)

Could it be done?

What might it do to my life if I tried?

Exhibitionist

I know perfectly well my own egotism,
Know my omnivorous lines and must not write any less

Staking a Claim

A MILE OF WRITING.

This is how I'd do it: expand my life at last, even while it continued to be bounded by town and the school run, morning and afternoon. On my home ground, inch by bloody inch. I wasn't able to wander my country like Whitman and all the other travelling writers I admired, so I must make something from my constraints instead. Stake a claim to a small, fixed spot under the youngest hornbeam tree beside the outdoor pool and be a prospector of stories, all spring and summer. What I'd done in private with hospice patients, I'd call forth now from swimmers and sunbathers, mining too my own memories of the wild and free.

How exciting it was. To have *an idea*. Thrilling as the first days of falling in love when you find yourself reciprocated, the universe seeming to see and smile on your desire.

Because everything fell into place, as if by magic, as soon as I dared in the cold December of my second out-of-work year to say what I wanted to do. One of the pool's directors was a former boss, who vouched for me so that a residency at the lido was soon announced in the regional press. And when I worried aloud in a first interview about finding a roll of paper as long as the pool, an architect got in touch to say the ones used by plotter printers for producing blueprints were just that length.

Then I did the maths. The pool used imperial measures and was advertised as fifty yards in length. Roughly a hundred and fifty feet or forty-five metres. To write a mile, I'd need to do thirty-five of what I'd call my *laps of longhand*. Too many horizontal lines to fit on a single scroll, so long yet so narrow. And so I'd use five rolls: one for each of the blue-edged swimming lanes, and with seven lengths of writing on every one. With the small and neat way I formed my letters, I calculated that I'd need to do a hundred thousand words: a novel-sized undertaking, all done by pen on paper in full view of swimmers.

I conducted all this odd planning with as much, or more, focus than I'd ever expended on paid work, conscientious though I'd always been. It came from a part of me never used before, operating without reference to anything except my own curiosity and will to make something that satisfied my sense of beauty. As birds are when working at their nests: nearest I can find to describe it.

With the purpose, the place and the paper all decided, I turned next to myself: how to transform in just a few months from a private person to a public one?

I became voracious then in my study of *women who had made their mark*. How did they do it? Distinguish themselves from all the other talented hundreds of thousands who made the attempt? Artists like Georgia O'Keeffe, Barbara Hepworth, Frida Kahlo. The outstanding movie stars: Garbo, Dietrich, Hepburn, Bacall. Our truly iconic writers: Woolf, Anaïs Nin, Simone de Beauvoir. As I'd once learned from Mother, dressing each morning for her admirers and critics alike, so now from these women.

I read their biographies, looking for patterns in how they spoke, the choices they made. Wrote out their boldest statements, making a playbook for how to take up space and claim attention as a woman artist. Analysed next their physical selves: Hepworth's overalls; O'Keeffe's almost monastic robes; Kahlo's colourful outfits; the mix of beauty and masculine poise in those early Hollywood women.

They all of them understood that a woman is always looked at, or overlooked. That to be a woman engaged in any public field is also to be a performer of womanhood. You are on show anyway, and so there is much to be gained from taking control of the stage, lights and wardrobe.

I assembled then my own costume – green headscarf, stained canvas apron with scarlet straps tied tight around my waist, old grey swimsuit with its burgundy halter neck cut low at the back. Painted my nails an ox-blood red so the hands that held my chin and pen would stand out against my brown skin and the white paper. Fetched a stepladder from the basement and stacked it with the books on water, place and nature I'd lend to all comers. Lifted my olive-green army kitbag onto my shoulder, heavy with my grandfather's utility-era coffee table with screw-in legs (what I'd played under as a child, and marked with my first crayoned letters).

Stood back to look in the mirror.

Yes. A portrait of the self-made artist. A curious blend of all the things that had ever compelled my imagination: aspects of ancient Japanese culture – part geisha, half monk; a provocation of bare skin balanced by the modesty of my covered hair; apron knotted at the side not the centre, as Mother had once taught me to do with brooches. Mix of many things, yet completely my own.

Before I wrote a single word in public, the first creative act had already taken place.

§

And of course the first day was awkward, and awful.

And the next. And the third when it rained, and I was the only person there, working under the bike shelter while wind blew my books off their stepladder. It was as if I'd fitted out a fancy new shop at great cost for the notice of no one. A friend I hadn't seen in a few years did call by to wish me luck but left within minutes. *How long would I have to stick it out?* she asked, looking both sceptical and sorry for me. *Five months? Every day?* She went away and didn't return.

But I kept going back, whatever the weather, affecting not to mind the unreadable looks of those who only watched from a distance.

Like the mirror I placed on the floor as a child, trying to make contact with God and my father. All the hours lying in fields pretending sleep and hoping to be found. As I held out grass to cows on the far side of the field from the bungalow. My long nights of learning quotes by heart for a few undergraduate exams. Resolving to turn early motherhood into an expedition. All these earlier exercises in persistence – even the hopeless ones, *especially those* – kept me knelt there, under the tree.

Some of the regular swimmers began to borrow my books.

A few began to recommend titles in turn, then bring them down as gifts for my makeshift library.

Then one morning the sculptor came to visit. Sitting on the grass across from me, he asked a few questions then understood everything. My reason for kneeling (a posture that recalled both prayer and the pillory: the stakes to which women are so often tied – purity, disgrace). The power of my being headscarved at work on a long piece of paper that was in the lineage of tapestries made by so many anonymous women going back through time. *Yes, yes.* And the scale of it, the absurd patience required. *Yes.*

Telling me then, before he went back to his own art, not to judge my success by how many people drew close. It was a tempting measure, but not the most important. It would be worth all my risk and effort, this huge and true display of . . . *vulnerability*, if it brought just *one decisive person* into my life (as my essay on the railings had connected him and me). He told me then how – as a still emerging artist in the seventies – he'd had a solo show in an obscure alternative London gallery. Nothing very likely to change his fortunes. But on a day of heavy rain, a curator from an American museum stumbled in on it by chance and a few years later included him in a show at the Guggenheim that lifted him to international prominence thereafter.

Once he was gone again, the paper no longer seemed so silly or resistant. I forgot my audience, or lack of it, and went down deep into my own stories, discovering there a powerful new dimension to what I was doing.

How had I not seen it till now? My mother's days had come alive for a while by marks made on paper: that rapid shorthand which caught every word from the mouth of her male boss. And through her rare skill, she gained entry for a while to the worlds of regional banking and local politics – little ponds, perhaps, but she felt herself a big fish at swim in them: all that was best in her being fully used and recognised. And now there I was, a half-century later, also using pen and paper to break open a larger life. What a heady, hardy feeling: to be reclaiming the stories of my female line and laying them out like brickwork – word by word, inch by inch. Building foundations for a legacy that just might last.

A Wild Woman

SO EVOCATIVE, THAT DESCRIPTION *of your young body and thoughts. I remember my own tanned limbs, bare feet and flip-flop lines . . .*

It was still only my first fortnight as artist-in-residence when I published a shy blog post that would alter everything. How exciting it was, with only a few dozen followers, to have a comment arrive on my phone like a bite on the line or a bright dragonfly alighting.

I peered at the blurry profile photo, taken underwater and showing mostly goggles, breath bubbles and tendrils of blond hair. Smiled then at the user name: *wildwomanswimming*.

Her next message was a private one. She had seen I was inviting submissions to an anthology of writing about water, and felt sure an extract from her online diaries would fit, after being polished up a bit.

But.

She was dying and already too ill to edit a selection for me. And it was a huge thing she was about to ask, she knew, but I'd been a hospice scribe, she was a paramedic, and we were both West Country women, so perhaps we could make a good team? *Work on her writing together, and talk too about living wild in the face of death?*

Yes, I said. Knowing that here she was, already. The sculptor had advised me to look out for this: the one life-changing person who'd respond to the signal I was sending out, day after day, like whale song.

Yes, I said to her, not thinking of what that answer would mean for me. *Yes*.

Such a strong undercurrent it created to my time beside the pool from then on, her incoming messages with their tidal reminder of how to live, how to die. Alongside myself, my mother and all the women of my line back to where the names were lost, here now was another female life to hold safe and honour.

Like me, the wild woman had been changed by serious illness. Turning to outdoor waters after breast cancer she was soon (being funny and physically fearless) at the heart of Devon's large wild swimming community. But now, balance problems had led to another shock diagnosis, and terminal this time.

Kneeling by the water, my skin and paper dappled by light, I still looked the very picture of ease and detachment. And yet there I was like Jacob with the angel, wrestling with matters of life and death once again as I copied the other woman's thoughts into my scrolls.

The treatment that's just finished was hard . . . I feel pinned to the bottom after a wipeout . . .

I want so much to think, to write it all out, talk about it, but I don't have the energy . . .

I found wild swimming at fifty, and things started to happen for me. Friendships built on adventure, art, writing . . .

Now the tumour has begun to make itself known, just as I felt I was finding my purpose. So where do I go now? I want to make meaning . . .

And then it came: her confession of regret. How hard to admit, she said, given how much skill, intelligence and talent for friendship she possessed: *I never found my place or people before now, and whenever I did arrive at something, I'd just drop it and move on, directionless. I wanted to write, but I diverted my energies always . . .*

Now it was too late. Not said, but clear to her and me both. And how precisely I knew the pain of that, so we arranged for me to visit her towards the end of summer when we'd begin work on her diaries – salvage something from her life's deepest desire, even if she didn't live to see the words reach readers.

§

The shadow of the wild woman dying back in the West Country cast my own late attempt at writing into even sharper relief, so that I became still more ambitious for it. That summer and those scrolls were my single best chance to create a lasting life as an artist, one that might begin to pay enough through grants or commissions to keep me outdoors for good.

And so I needed to amplify my quiet presence beside the pool. Just as O'Keeffe came to prominence as a painter when her lover Stieglitz exhibited her canvases alongside exquisite nudes he'd made of her, so I must create an iconography for my work: images that could travel beyond the brick and flint walls of the pool and make strangers stop their online scrolling to look, then read.

But to seek and brief a photographer was a terribly shy exercise for an ignored daughter grown old. To have a man pay me close attention had always been my dearest wish, but to ask for it? As difficult to voice as the wild woman had found her end-of-life regrets.

There was just one person I felt able to approach: a father who'd had children in the same nursery as my own, whose family photographs shared on social media were lit so that the everyday seemed infused with a sacred aspect. A loving husband and a proud parent of daughters, I admired his manner too – the kind of man I'd have liked to be raised by, if such choice were ever given.

Like the sculptor, he understood within moments everything I was trying to achieve, saying yes to me as swiftly as I had to the wild woman. There was a condition, though: he wouldn't charge for his time, but I did need to hand him my whole trust, setting aside any received ideas of my best angle, a pleasing smile. Yes?

Yes, I said, it being my season of agreeing to strange bargains for the hopeful feeling, light as thistledown, that came from making them.

How at ease he made me feel, so that I felt able to say what even Nye didn't know: that each time my father drove past me, unheeding, in the small town where I'd lived, I felt myself a stray dog or a piece of litter. That I fell into compensatory dreams of being an object of use or beauty – a jug of hedgerow flowers on a tablecloth, a willow-pattern plate. And so these scrolls and my kneeling to them was not only a response to my near-death and wish to live more vividly ever since, but also – at a far deeper level – a chance to *remake* myself. To assume my right size and shape at last. To claim authority. *To be seen.* Did he understand?

He did, entrusting to me stories of his own childhood as we began work, so I could laugh and feel natural despite our unusual business. Conversation, my comfort zone.

But then, with our hours of filming almost at their end, he asked me simply to stand still, and straight, against a white wall. To look unsmiling into the lens, naked of make-up.

I'd already floated, face to the sky, and swum laps while he filmed me from underwater. Had knelt at my scrolls, pen in hand, before shaking out a length of the paper like laundry. Bizarre things, all in view of pool-goers. This should have been the work of minutes, and yet it triggered in me a backwash of old miseries: all the many times I'd hated my face in a mirror or my body in clothes.

How much I wanted to end the session then, breaking my promise.

(Oh these brief but decisive moments when we step from shame into whatever lies on the other side. Each one never easier than the last.)

'Give me a moment, I can feel tears coming. This is horribly hard. Look away, will you?' I had to close my eyes then, bending over to ready myself. Diver on a high board.

'OK. Let's go.'

It was only a camera, a man, and me in middle age. But the sensation was one of freefall, release. A corset torn off and thrown aside.

The writing continued steadily after this as before but the woman doing it parted ways with doubt, deference, disguise. No more being modest, playing small.

I had learned, so late, to stand unadorned and look the world in the eye. To see and be seen in an equal exchange of gazes.

How wild I felt, how free.

§

Something of my new confidence proved magnetic. I'd been curled over my paper like a question mark from the beginning, but it was only now that people gathered round to give me their stories. So many, so fast, that each day felt like a week or more of my old life. After decades of holding back and hiding, with so few people to know my private passions, now I was out in the open. The girl who'd turned away at the gate of the pool party, and had envied her mother's bedtime stories of naked moonlit swims: she was bare-soled and wide awake. On show.

And what did this bold display call forth in others? Confessions and cautionary tales about things surprisingly intimate: size and shape; status and security; speed and distance. *How many of us were carrying this sense of weight or weightlessness.* What I began to understand as I listened to hundreds of strangers confide their inner lives each week. Always believing ourselves too big, too small, too old, too timid, too poor for our time and place. How would it be if the mass of us could lay that burden down and acquire a sense of *right fit*, feeling at home in our skins, our stories?

'Pension funds love middle managers.'

I looked up from my writing to a man who could have been an extra in *The Swimmer*, that unnerving film of outdoor pools and suburban excess. Barrel-chested as Burt Lancaster, and in the same tiny trunks, he stood hands on hips, in a halo of sun.

'You're writing about life and death, yes? The wild and free? Really living?'

I nodded, putting down my pen.

'Well listen to this. I'm an actuary. Do you know what that is?'

I nodded again, shielding my eyes against the glare.

'Write this down. What the figures reveal. Men in professions always work *ten years too long*. They don't want to lose their social standing and are desperate for the best pension possible – but . . . they die soon after retirement! Within five years on average! The funds make so much money from them! This is why I'll be stopping at fifty-five to find a part-time job in a supermarket or garden centre. It's better to earn less and live longer. *Tell all the men you meet here . . .*'

'I've had cancer, and haven't swum since.' A woman who had come to the pool, she said, after finding my flyer in the bookshop. 'The doctor says it's safe again but . . .' She stopped, and held her jumper close to her throat.

'But you are a different shape now?' I said. 'Weigh more?'

Yes. She nodded. Was serious, then brightened. 'As a fellow member of the near-death club, you'll just tell me to get the hell in the pool, won't you?'

Yes. I nodded, we laughed. She swam. First time in five years.

'How fit you are!' What I said in admiration to a man who came to dry next to me. He pointed to some marks on his thigh. Injections. Multiple sclerosis, and gaining on him fast. He had been trying to outswim it, but perhaps it was time to keep kinder company with his condition?

I looked away from him at all the people in the crowded lanes and got a feeling akin to the bends. The pressure of so many lives in that small patch of water. Their private burdens.

Feeling so newly at ease in my own self, I wished then – as I had at the hospice – for secular versions of spiritual rites. Because I'd happily grow old and ragged beside the pool if immersing people there day after day could free them of unease, as baptismal waters promise to wash us clean of sin.

Border Disputes

THERE CAME THEN JUST A FEW balmy weeks in which I performed a trick with time so that each minute of every hour became rich and lambent as bottled fruit.

The weather was warm, and the raucous school holiday season not yet begun; the soundtrack was water lapping at the pool's tiled edges and the song of a blackbird that owned a nearby lamp post; the air was scented by bare skin and freshly laundered towels. And so many people were beginning to visit, bees to the flowers of me and my books: swimmers from other lidos, local artists, aspiring writers, all of them coming to sit beneath the hornbeam tree.

But even while I worked to create a magical space apart from normal time, the outside world kept intruding.

As I began to attract more attention – local papers, regional TV, national radio, magazine features – the way existing friends and acquaintances spoke to me began to curdle into something hard to swallow.

'Still scribbling away?'

'Aren't you lucky to have a husband who will look after the children on weekends so you can be here at the pool?'

'I'd love to spend so much time on a *hobby*.'

How ants will squirt acid if their nest is disturbed – this was that. My art, being made in the open instead of a gallery space, was an irritant – a small disturbance in the way things worked. Its purpose, too, was obscure – being done for reasons other than the usual currencies of payment or publication – and therefore unsettling to those investing in cars, house extensions, school fees, foreign holidays. It didn't add up.

There was only one exchange that truly hurt, and worked poison, thorn-like.

One of my closest friends was a much older woman I'd met in the park when my son was still only a few months old. Since then she had helped me raise both my children, and I loved her dearly. So I listened, smiling at first, when she said that she'd seen me stride through the shopping precinct in my costume of headscarf and paint-stained apron. I was anticipating something only funny or fond from her.

'You looked like you owned the place! A man sitting next to me at the bus stop nudged my arm and said: *See her! Looks like she needs to be put in the bath and given a damn good scrub!*'

'Did you say that you knew me, and I was an artist?' I asked, my jaw and stomach aching, as if I'd been force-fed something sour.

No, she hadn't. Truth was, she agreed. My new way of dressing and spending my days were a pity, she felt. I'd been such a good housekeeper before, like her; now I reminded her of women from her run-down wartime neighbourhood: *They all had filthy pinnies too – using them to wipe up spills, then faces. She'd never been able to stand a dirty apron.*

There it was, old predator. *Shame.* The physical clench and heat that happens when it comes close, sniffing at how shabby, smelly, stupid we are. The nakedness when enduring its gaze so that we want afterwards to hide our face, and be blanket-wrapped, with curtains shut. Hidden, safe.

This was only my own discomfort, and chosen. I'd been wanting, after all, and for a long time, to test the limits of small-town life after being taught since earliest childhood that the most important thing for me as a working-class girl and woman was my *good reputation.* To be respectable and beyond reproach in the eyes of my neighbours: as important as any court of law.

But then, in just the second month of my experiment, far darker and more dangerous forces began breaking loose in public so that I put aside the private and personal aspect of my work. I'd begun by only braiding together my own memories, stories from pool-goers and daily nature notes; now the scrolls became a seismograph, recording the shock waves travelling through the political system and our streets.

I was writing beside the pool when a female member of Parliament at her constituency office was shot by a man shouting 'Britain First'. Stunned sunbathers kept coming over with their phones, wanting me – their scribe – to record their anger, their sadness, at the horrifying developments. *Stabbed. Kicked. Critical. Dead.*

I was writing there the next day when young children sat near me after school eating ice lollies and microwaved chips while tallying in worried whispers which of their classmates' mothers and fathers might soon be *sent home.*

I was writing there on the day when I, like other British citizens, could only vote *yes* or *no* on a complex question that would affect generations; a day when newspapers were placed on towels like banners of allegiance, and it became difficult for any of us to speak and not declare our colours.

Here and now. A repeating phrase I'd begun to use as anchor, as safety line, to recall me to the present moment of the pool whenever worries about the country began to overwhelm.

A man doing laps of breaststroke spits out water, loudly; a woman does a fast front crawl with hardly a sound; two girls play at synchronised swimming.

I sketched the day in words, began to breathe again. But then a couple stopped inches from my paper and zipped themselves into wetsuits.

'We're getting ready for the nuclear war!' One of them called to me, laughing.

A time of border disputes, then. Ugly, uneasy.

As without, so within: my new incarnation beginning to cause friction with Nye.

Our first big row happened when I rose very early one Friday like a fisherman to dress for an attempt at a whole twelve hours on show.

How happy I was, how full of energy.

My boiled eggs were rattling in their pan, rations for the long day ahead, and I smiled to be padding about in the house while the rest of the family were sleeping – all was calm, all was bright. A Christmas-morning feeling although it was before six on a July day already blue and warm as a gas flame. I went back to the bedroom for my apron and Nye opened one eye.

'What on earth are you doing?'

And I might have been politic, soothing, if only in a tactical way, for expedience. Instead, I bridled, as if his words were reins and bit between my teeth.

'Excuse me?'

I reminded him that he was taking a day off so I could work all day for once: that a writer might be coming from London to put me in her book, and a group of swimmers travelling down from another county—

Ridiculous. How excessive. And had I told the children last night that I'd be away all day?

I swore in a whisper and said, going out, that he was trying to yoke me to that old gender role: mother hen.

And then I came back and said everything I'd been holding in.

Had he not left the house unannounced every weekday in this first decade of child-rearing to catch whatever train he chose, directed only by his meeting schedule? Why might I not have just a few Fridays and my weekends through this unrepeatable season to take my fences, riderless? To see how far and fast I could go without the weight of the house, the children?

For the last three years, we'd had a shared conceit that I'd become – since leaving the office – a hawk, a hunting bird, red in tooth and claw. A wild, free thing that came only to his hand. An idea which suited our stock of images, all quasi-medieval – how we'd always been happiest living a routine, rooted life organised, like an illustrated book of hours, around husbandry. The care of our garden, our young, our elders. We joked that I dropped people and their stories into the marriage, warm and vivid as field mice, while he fed us a steady supply of monthly income like honey. But I resented now the idea of being kept on a line – however light – that was stopping me going as high and far as I wanted.

We love one another through language as much as touch, and it is in words where the gaps are forming: fault lines.

What I wrote to him from my better self when I was away at the pool, able to see things more clearly without our home around me.

Yes, I thought. It is as if the fairy-tale scale of my labour had begun to exact the price of all myth and fable: once one feels to have it all, at last, precisely then is when it starts to strain and crack.

Fox Woman Dreaming fills the woodcutter's desolate cottage with her company and cooking smells – *sex, joy, increase!* – but he complains about her own sharp stink until she goes away and he is alone again.

The selkie may leave the water and bear a son with the lonely boatman – but her body begins to insist on the sea: her skin thins and flakes; her eyes, hair and teeth go dull and discoloured. It hurts to stay on land and love, but to leave is loss and sorrow.

Give me one summer, I wrote on the back of one of my own flyers. *Where, apart from evening care of our children, I am accountable for nothing. No meal-making, social planning or small talk. Let me live on eggs, apples and carrots, and stay up till two a.m. and rise at six in a separate room.*

When I returned in the late evening, and handed it him to read, he said *yes, sorry, of course* and yet I felt his heart murmur *stay, don't go* so I climbed in under the covers and pretended for a long while to be sleeping beside his soon-sleeping self. But I could feel the sands of my miraculous public summer running, running, running out – there simply wasn't *time* to be inside.

In Heat

OFF THE PILL AND WITH MY WEDDING RING thrown away in temper, I sat sleepless in the attic. New and unhappy night-time routine since midsummer when I felt the season begin sliding towards the pool's September closing day.

Nye and the children were in separate rooms on the floors below, but I was still crowded, caged. Like a vixen in heat, I wanted to be outside the house, skirting fields and fences, laying scent trails, lying in wait. Not sitting spinster-neat on a single bed, hemmed in by the books of bolder women: Anaïs Nin noting in her diary that all days should be so good – the sperm of seven men by bedtime; Frida Kahlo lying laughing on the grass with a female lover; Lee Miller posing naked for the camera of Man Ray, equals in bed and art; Georgia O'Keeffe likewise with Stieglitz; Simone de Beauvoir delighting in a first orgasm at almost forty, just as she'd been resigning herself to losing youth and beauty.

'It's like a veil has been lifted.' What an earnest friend had said to me at the end of our twenties, she having stopped her contraception in the months before marriage. 'I am smelling men, everywhere. *Seeing them.* Their shape, how they move. Wanting their weight.' Sex had been in the head till now, she suspected; driven by a wish to be admired, coupled up. *How appalling*, we agreed, if the very thing we'd taken to prevent pregnancy since our teens had, all along, been a kind of *chemical veil*. Taming and containing us like the hood on a hawk or cloth laid over a birdcage. Putting to sleep our wilder desires. *God. How awful.* But we turned away from where it might have led us, such knowledge, and continued going from shop to costly shop looking at finishing touches for her fast-approaching ceremony and reception.

Now, arriving at a creative life in my mid-forties, I was newly off the pill for the same reason I knelt each day to confront yard after yard of blank paper: *to see what I was made of.* I wanted to learn my monthly ebb and flow and use it to propel my writing in those last years before the menopause and the unchosen changes it would make to the body I'd been born to.

So I could rise fast each morning for my work at the pool, I'd also stopped the sleeping tablets I'd been taking since the emergency and its damage, and this only added to the raw nature of my wakefulness. A flood of strong hormones. Nerve pain. New estrangement from Nye. All these made for uneasy nights at home, but I accepted them as the price of my enlivened days.

When I did reach dream, I was often now a woman turned beast. Brought to all fours by an unseen force, and with my tendons straining at their new shape, I suffered being sewn into a wolfskin and driven from town. Running then, for hours, leagues; chased, escaping; low to the ground and tasting the air. Making a repeating pattern in the soil of three paws and a single handprint: the one that writes, which I found between my legs on waking.

It was to do with sex in its unmannered, amoral form, the sort that makes for the gap in the fence, forgetting the fold – what a feminist writer from an earlier era called *the zipless fuck*: the fantasy of having it anywhere, often, with anyone, at no cost to family or social standing (although there is always a cost if one loves and belongs).

But it was also about power. Range and expansion of territory. Energy. Appetite. Ambition.

And this made me monstrous, of course. That I was a woman not simply glad of a few schoolday and weekend hours in which to write politely, but one who wanted *more time, more time, more.*

At the pool the next day, I shivered in the sun, while the hand that supported my chin felt naked. Its ring finger a mollusc, unshelled; white and damp and shrunken in the place where the band had always been.

Soul Swims Wild

IN MY OWN RAW HUNGER FOR MORE TIME, I'd forgotten how little was left to the wild woman.

And now a message came through from another member of her swimming community to recall me to the promise I'd made. The brain tumour had returned despite chemo and surgery, the friend said, and was growing now *at a fearsome rate* – mere cells to the size of a cricket ball in just a few weeks. The wild woman had been fast-tracked into a hospice for end-of-life care, and wanted it written about, insisting that there was someone ready to do it.

I think she might mean you? wrote this other woman. *Your timeline says you're due back in the West Country mid-August. Would you be willing to visit her then?*

Yes, I said. *Of course.*

But then the first words in weeks came through from the wild woman herself: *yesitaabDtinebur I anbeunghekpwd. Wouldlovetomeet inpersonfinfong writing hard.*

'Look,' I said to Nye, showing him my screen. 'August will be too late.'

So at four in the morning on our late-July wedding anniversary we bundled our sleeping children and swim things into the car and set off on a six-hour drive to the West Country. Yet another weight I was laying onto our marriage.

§

She woke from sleep and I fell for her, this woman I'd taken care not to research online so as not to be shocked upon our meeting by her diminishment. I needn't have worried: her charisma travelled in waves across the room to where I stood in the doorway – palpable even before we took each other by the hands to exclaim at their being the same broad shape. *Our shared farming heritage, look, though we'd never met till now!*

Shaven-headed, swollen by medicine and lopsided in her chair, she was terribly, terribly ill.

But also superb. And *all there*, taking charge of our talk as soon as I'd straightened her and chosen a chair for myself.

'I read that you had a late post-partum haemorrhage?'

Her first question to me, paramedic to her bones. I nodded, glad to have got straight to the matters of life and death that had brought me there.

'Of everything I dealt with in the service, that was the worst: the mothers I drove away from their homes, bleeding out.'

She told me then visceral details of how she'd worked to slow their blood loss – horrific to hear for most people, but to me it was like a poultice applied to the part of myself that relived it every anniversary (*my annual return to the trenches*: how I described it when retreating from company each November). The wild woman's words – with their frank naming of what I'd endured – were like the laying on of hands. *Hurt: be gone.*

This was her unexpected gift to me.

Mine to her was also a story.

Because beyond regret at leaving a life she loved, with her writing unpublished, there was also a fear of pain that none of her vast reading had assuaged. *She'd seen so much of it . . .*

'But remember,' I said, 'you were always called to accidents and emergencies. I once witnessed a quieter dying.'

'Tell me, please,' she said, bracing herself, hands on the arms of her wing-backed chair.

So I did. Vertiginous with the richness of life, and the line of chance events in mine that were knitting now into a thing of use and beauty. The lost girl that was me at eighteen doing night shifts in care homes: she had a story tailor-made for this woman, here, years later.

A SILK STOCKING

Back there, back then, I'd been in the basement laundry one night, ironing and folding as always, when the senior assistant – an Eastern European woman who took pride in laying out the bodies – came to find me. It was a full moon, she said, and the residents were unsettled. It took them that way. Would it frighten me to sit with one who'd likely die that night? She understood that in this country few people my age had seen it happen.

And that was how I came to spend the unearthly hours of one until four in the morning holding a small hand, smooth and light as a rabbit paw. The room was hot as a dormouse nest, and the tiny woman inside it seeming only to hibernate. But then, without any struggle, her breaths began to come further apart. I felt the skin change before I understood the heart and lungs had stopped: she went loose and gossamer-smooth, like a silk stocking left on the bed. *A body no longer clothing soul . . .*

'Thank you,' said the wild woman when I finished.

And she remembered then that pneumonia used to be called *the widow's friend* – what elderly folk always wished for because of the peace it could bestow on one's ending. *Perhaps, with luck, she might go that way too?*

Less than a month later, it was. In the early hours of an August morning – when I was already up after a disturbed night, readying for a second long drive to her – she died in her sleep, aged fifty-five, with her mother holding her hand.

Driving away from the hospice to the coastal town where we'd be spending the next few days, I sat in the passenger seat and began to read her online diaries. There hadn't been time before.

I knew she'd written them quickly after each adventure, often with her hair still wet, so I was nervous of their quality. But she was a natural. So much life and love – for friends, place, nature – and all done in language that darted from the lyrical to bawdy and back again.

'Listen,' I kept saying to Nye. 'Listen.'

My soul swims wild: just one of the many beautiful phrases I underlined as we drove. This was writing that deserved far more than a short extract in an anthology with only a small print run, locally sold.

But I'd never worked in publishing. The collection of others' words I was to make over winter would, I was sure, be pamphlet-plain and hardly read beyond a few pool-goers. Who was I to midwife her work, or persuade an editor to take it? And the timing was bad, terrible. I'd only spent a few months on my own late and grandiose art work. *How could I bear to give so much time to someone else, when I'd only just made this space for my own creative life?*

And yet.

The thought of rendering a service of such size for no reward other than its rightness: this had a density to it, a gravitational pull – a siren call beckoning me, against reason, into another of the boundary states I'd been seeking ever since the near-death.

I looked then at Nye in profile. His beautiful dark curls of long ago had become hair cropped close now and almost white. His face still dear to me, even though we'd begun to bicker daily over my new life.

Hadn't it been like this for us all those years ago? Our meeting bringing us to a sudden need to *choose*. And whatever dropped away when we joined our fates back then, that didn't weigh now on the scales, whereas what we'd made together – a home, children, our shared married language – *did*.

As with him, so with the wild woman. I would lend my life to hers at its ending, and not count the cost. And so I began to say titles aloud under my breath until I found the one that had a ring to it. *Wild Woman Swimming: A Journal of West Country Waters*. Yes. After the scrolls, this is what I'd do next. Somehow.

Strange but true: there was a honeymoon mood between Nye and me for the rest of the trip, despite the seriousness of what we'd set out to do and the arguments that had lately begun between us.

It was like the best dreams I've had of him and me through the years, in which we stand always at a tideline, laughing, while turtles and lobsters roll in on blood-warm waves to our feet – soul symbols, I suppose, of good fortune, natural treasure.

There is a photo of us sharing the hotel mirror on that anniversary evening, admiring ourselves. His paid work was feeling newly important, he said, after brushing his teeth and rinsing, because it freed me to go open-hearted through the world in a way that he, introvert, never could. I kissed him, put on my lipstick and mascara. We laughed about being Donald Sutherland and Julie Christie in our favourite film: sexy like them in that Venice bathroom, though we had children beyond the door. Moving, as they did, in that synchronised way the long-coupled have. Talking side by side while doing what are usually private ablutions. *Pee, wipe, brush, spit*. How close we were still, I am trying to say. Married in gesture and rhythm as well as law.

And we enjoyed radiant hours with the children, too, at a sea pool we went to after the hospice. Swimming in thick brine among jellyfish, crab, kidney-red anemones, gelatinous green seaweed. Sitting then by pastel-coloured changing huts eating ice creams. Bare feet, big jumpers, tousled hair. The cine-reel version of family life I'd been without in my own growing: *mother, father, brother, sister*. Our car loaded with flasks, blankets, buckets, spades. Glorious Technicolor. The stuff of love.

Lover of Unreason

O something unprov'd! something in a trance!
To escape utterly from others' anchors and holds!
To drive free! to love free! to dash reckless and dangerous!
To court destruction

A Wren's Tale

A RAGGED MAIDEN ARRIVES AT THE THRESHOLD of a castle or cottage, advancing then in small steps towards the heart of the house and her story. She comes in from the cold to find a place provisioned for comfort: food for hunger, stove for warmth.

This scene which recurs so often in fairy tales, preceding rest on a borrowed bed: what need, bone-deep in us, does it stand for? It speaks, I believe, to a longing for *ease* and *relief*, and is an exchange old as our social customs: security for the woman who is lost, or cast out, or escaping; company for the lonely fellow who is cut off by work, or curse, or character. She is without the protection of maleness; he, immured by it. And their encounter, and the mating and merging of souls which follows from it? It promises a miracle cure for all that is aching or asleep in each of them: the girl who knocks, and the man or beast who answers.

The mile of writing was going to take two summers, not one, I had realised quite early on in my undertaking, and so winter was a limbo in which I had too much time to wonder how I'd summon the nerve and energy to begin again when the pool reopened in May.

I was also concerned that the scrolls should not be my one and only performance piece. And this is what brought me in the cold new year to the door of a stranger's workshop in a distant village, bearing a shy sketch of the art installation I dreamed of but could never make myself: a life-size version of my childhood's lost barometer with all its moving parts.

I came with only a name, address and recommendation, holding no advance image of this person who was without an online life – one of those vanishingly rare craftsmen employed always without need to advertise. And all my attention and strength had anyway been needed that day simply to dress, and drive out from town, and walk down a lane, through a gate, then a garden, and stand straight to knock on the door and wait. I wasn't thinking about who might be behind it, being full instead of worry about how difficult these simplest things had become. Dressing. Driving. Walking.

I was really very ill, wasn't I?

What I admitted in the long minutes while that door stayed shut. The many vivid hours beside the pool through the previous spring, summer and early autumn: they'd made me rich in reputation and new friendships, but at a cost to my health, as well as my marriage. Through all the winter months soon ending, more and more odd symptoms had been taking hold: confusion, loss of appetite, heart pains, fainting halfway home from even short walks for groceries. (*How breathless I was now, just standing still.*) I kept visiting doctors, begging for help, but there was nothing they could find.

And as my body was failing, so was I in my second life.

My other understanding, as I waited at a door that recalled my father's which had remained closed to me since my eleventh year. Over the phone before Christmas, Mother had said in passing that he had cancer – what someone in town had told her, anyway. Since then the daily hurt of my early years had returned. I was waiting, I think, for the call or letter that would likely come from him, so late, when even the birthday cards with a five-pound note left for me on Granny's sideboard had stopped at sixteen; how he'd be expecting me to help him ease his conscience before dying. *And what would I do then?* Ignore him? Say something punishing? Ask him to explain what I'd never understood? Could I forgive him, even? Did I have that in me?

I'd worked so hard since my near-death to get free of the narrow way of living that childhood loss had created in me. And I'd succeeded, on the surface: the scrolls had earned me acclaim, redeeming my name from being only one I shared with the man who'd abandoned me – my circles of belonging were far larger now. But they hadn't rescued me – *not at all* – from the stray feeling I'd confessed to the photographer. If anything, all my determined efforts to remake myself in my own image, as if I'd sprung from a field or flower instead of Father, it had only brought me back to my self's secret shame: *no man had ever loved me, and no man ever would.* (Nye had been a boy when we met, and we'd grown up together, so that the girl in me – resistant to logic – was still yearning, stubbornly, for the love of an older man.)

There I was, then, disquieted, on a stranger's doorstep. My old navy raincoat letting in the cold, with me feeling just as threadbare. Worn thin with experience. I'd just received word of a residency in Switzerland promised me for September (four miraculous, well-paid weeks), and yet the time I'd have to cross before reaching the rest it represented? *An impossible distance.* I needed, already, urgently, a place of peace and quiet away from unhappiness at home and the public gaze which had left me feeling X-rayed, all exposed bone (the pool was shut now but people kept stopping me in the streets, asking questions whenever I sat at a café table or park bench – I was famous, for those few seasons, in one small place).

The door opened, and I stepped inside.

Woman become wren.

What happened when I followed that man into his work space. *Colour. Form. Texture.* A bower. While he finished a phone call, back turned after showing me in, I chose a chair and perched there, neat and drab and noticing.

His voice, the shape of him, his dark hair: how all this affected me.

And how many small objects in his rooms had their mates in mine! Before a word was exchanged, I had intuited the huge and hidden hinterland of what we'd find in common.

Afterwards, when we had shaken hands on a deal – he agreeing to work with me on proper plans and then build the Weather House should I ever get funding – after this, as I was going away again down the lane, my own voice, catching me unawares: *I will be the woman of this place.*

I stopped, putting my hand around my throat, too late to snare it. Phrase from a version of FOX WOMAN DREAMING ('What,' a teller of it once said, 'all women long to say, and men to hear.')

Loneliness of the
Long-Distance Writer

YES, I REALLY WAS VERY ILL.

Between my first visit to the stranger on that February day and my next a month later, I would cross a very different threshold: a hospital emergency ward where I was wheeled within minutes to an isolation room, on the brink of sepsis: a silent kidney infection that had spread to other organs. Lungs, bladder, stomach – my whole self slow-poisoned by the strain of kneeling hour after hour, day after month, while exposed to so much sun and curiosity.

Yet another bedside scene for Nye and me, but there was no tender reuniting this time. My poor health was now becoming a logistical difficulty for us, and another of the things for which we could find no common language in this hardest year of our long marriage.

I'm in a dark root garden.

What Nye said when I went down to the basement at two a.m. after another Saturday night reading alone in bed, while he played at the computer game that had held him spellbound for months. It was spring now, and I knew with the change to the weather that I was coming to care very much for the man in the far-off workshop – my immediate sense that I was *always supposed to have known him* having only deepened at each of our weekly meetings.

And I wanted to save myself, and the marriage, so came downstairs hoping to solve this problem of my divided heart without Nye needing to know of it.

Unfair test and a fool's errand.

I can't find a way past this gatekeeper.

Said with his back turned to me, in the same voice he might have used in a happier time to confide a tricky work meeting or the potato crop failing in the back garden.

Cracked round shield. Wanderer boots. Balder leggings.

He scrolled through an inventory of equipment and I began to see the gravity of the game. Dense with effort and purpose, its economy was serious – a trading in souls. He had just today, he told me, become fully human after starting as a hollow man.

Collecting herbs, mixing spells, breaking horses, building houses, all while the fabric of our own home frayed: how strange that the dreams of the man I'd slept beside for twenty years were most likely not of work or family but this castle and its endless battlements.

He began then to run through a forest in which the trees attacked at every turn, and I said Dante from memory, those lines Nye and I had learned together in my distant undergraduate days:

> *Midway upon the journey of our life*
> *I found myself within a forest dark,*
> *For the straightforward pathway had been lost.*

I thought he might be reminded of that other time, and smile, and turn to me, but he didn't. Instead: a standoff. *The game was creative, and requiring of skill*, he said, humourless. I disagreed, unpleasant, from my high horse. *However much one feels to have run miles or fought hard with sword or bow, nothing has been changed by it. No muscles or true aim have been developed.*

He looked at me then. Cold eyes, hard mouth. Saying that work and the children were enough for him. There was nothing wrong with just passing time in between. *We couldn't all be bulbs burning bright.* And my time in Switzerland couldn't come quickly enough for him. Why didn't I ask them to take me sooner so I could be with my *own kind*?

Marriage as a matter of weights and measures: a couple can be calibrated on a scale unlike everyone around them, even while they appear to run on the same principles as their family and friends. Ours, I remembered now and so late, had always been organised around growth and learning. He taught me, and I him. Now, as I advanced into the open with my knowledge, he was retreating into Lego, TV shows. Child's play that bonded him to our son and daughter just as they were forgetting the fun I'd improvised for them out of cloth, bubbles and buttons in their early years.

I might have been kinder, and more careful to have shared my new days instead of escaping into them. And he might have let me grow and go with better grace. Instead we had become now the Weather House couple: me outside, on show, beyond the point of safety; him in shadow, determined to hibernate.

The Weather Breaks

DID I EVER MOVE OR SLEEP? What a boy shivering inside his towel wanted to know.

'What do you eat?' asked the girl beside him, gap-toothed and freckled, as she leaned over to take a spider from my hair.

'Well . . .' I put my hands either side of my mouth to show I was telling them something not just anyone could know. 'Unless *kind children* feed me, then the same awful things every day: boiled eggs, apples, carrots . . .'

They ran off laughing to find their parents and ask for treats to offer me, *Lady Who Lives Under the Tree*.

Oh, how easy it would be to stop here and go no further into the artist's life. What I thought then. How much I had loved this self-created undertaking and the way it had brought me into close contact with so many good new people. And what a relief to have worked loose from the double binds woven around wives and mothers. But such a burden I'd placed on my marriage and existing friendships in the meanwhile. Better now, perhaps, to fade after this second and last summer into one of the town's eccentrics who were spoken of with fondness not alarm. Like the gone-now university lecturer who went always along the same badger tracks for his daily walk – head full of Eliot and the Bible, arms behind his back and clasped at the wrists, trousers held up with string. Him and others of that kind still living, who in their unvarying routines and odd costumes were a sort of communal resource: one of the ways we could all feel belonging, through recognition and a shared set of references.

But no, I wasn't ready yet for that. To have broken free from respectability so late only to settle for being a sideshow, a mild amusement? No.

Earlier that morning, I'd felt close to the geisha-like life I'd dreamed of as an overlooked child. It was a day of national celebration for writing, and many swimmers had accepted my challenge to compose a letter, so wherever I looked people were deep in concentration. The poolside tree I worked under had been newly decorated with paper streamers by a visiting school, using strips which they'd covered – again at my invitation – with words for water.

A Shinto shrine! said a woman walking past who'd travelled to Japan as I hadn't. As she said it, my sense of pleasure and purpose shrank into shame: I was only playing at a way of being I wasn't born to, and hadn't even seen as a tourist. *There was so much I still hadn't done.*

At the end of that long heatwave day, in the minutes before thunder came and lightning happened, I began a short message of my own. A parting note to the man in the hidden studio, now our work together had just ended. THE WEATHER BREAKS, I typed into the subject line before pressing send. And a second later, it did.

§

The seasons of love. How it moves through them, announcing its arrival.

Small and steady taps like a thrush at a snail shell. What the other admires, defends, dislikes. Little stories traded at the end of a work meeting. Being shown a photo of a boy on a beach by the man he has become and wishing to be that shy child's mother, sister, friend: playmate and protector of their earlier, irrecoverable self. Watching a pen cross a page and wanting those marks and the hand making them to be *perpetual*, always at the edge of one's vision.

My other love. How I'd begun to think of that man since early spring without giving a single outward sign of how I felt. It was simply a disaster of impossible feeling – a landslip, a sinkhole opened up – that I must contain and cover over. And it was easy to do, his behaviour being only ever professional, polite, friendly. Each time we sat down to consider the dream house I hoped to make material, our hours passed fast in a blur of research until I was once again shaking his hand in thanks on the doorstep before going away.

There'd only been one moment when we tipped into talk that opened onto another dimension. A small oil painting had appeared on one of his walls since my last visit, a view of nearby Mount Caburn done in rough golds and browns, and when I saw the signature I called out to him in another room.

'You have a Trekkie!'

He came to stand beside me, closer than we'd ever sat together at his workbench, and we looked at it together. He'd only just chosen it, he said, for the view, but didn't know much about the artist yet.

'I have her letters,' I said, excited. 'Hers and Leonard Woolf's.' Telling him then how they'd become companions after Virginia's death. A few polite notes about coming to his London home for tea, toast and boiled eggs and then it somehow deepened into *a lifelong arrangement.* She remaining married to her husband, while dividing her time between the two men for the rest of Leonard's life.

I had put my hand on his arm while saying all this, forgetting myself, and the day seemed to tilt a little: that capsizing sensation of falling in love when you are not free for it. But then, after that single touch of his sleeve, we stepped apart and said our now usual farewell on the doorstep. I wanted our work to be over then, and done, while dreading too its ending.

Even now, months later, I'd no hope of reciprocation. And so my message had been brief in its wording, and courteous. I asked for nothing and regretted only that I would not be calling by again. I'd arrived as a stranger and would leave missing his company.

§

Just days after those careful words I'd written on a brittle heat-wave evening, I was back in that studio where I had no business to be any more. And the man it belonged to who'd only ever shaken my hand until then was now pressing my palm to his chest so I could feel how hard and fast his heart beat beneath his clothes.

A visit of minutes.

Because he was going away soon, as I would be too – there was simply no *time* to make sense of where we found ourselves. And so it seemed that morning as if we were only holding something between us for a moment, before sending it *away away* to safety: this love I'd brought to his door, dazed and frightened, like the body of a bird collided with a wall or window.

In his reply to my note, he'd spoken of *his careful emotional architecture*. His need for order, and space. How hard he was to reach, to know. Yet, he didn't, *no*, want me to stay away from his door after this. Mightn't we – once we were back in autumn – find some way to be together that didn't threaten my people or his?

But. Yet. Although.

I drove away from him, rabbit fast, mind spinning from being neither rejected nor embraced. The hedges were looming twice their usual size. Too wild, too alive.

Love in Double Time

BLACKBIRDS, BRINGERS OF GOOD NEWS.

A sketch made and sent to me from a foreign clifftop. We'd agreed to maintain radio silence until autumn, he and I, after that brief and confusing moment in his workshop before he had to leave the country. We'd meet again in October, somewhere outdoors, on my return from the Swiss residency – begin then to find a safe outlet for this huge affection and need for one another's company that we'd now both admitted.

But with these words from him, just days after we'd parted, it began already. A summer-long courtship conducted mostly in writing, even while I still had to work daily on the scrolls, so that I was a woman living in language – the rest of my life pushed to the margins. We exchanged in this way our whole childhood histories, as bower and dowry: all the lives we'd held dear back then, and now as adults; how we loved this landscape we'd neither of us been born in, but wanted never to leave; the miles of it we'd explore together, sharing to this end maps and co-ordinates: where we'd sit, eat, rest.

Each day becoming a concentrate, drunk neat, in double time, so that we hadn't chance to eat or sleep. Everything read or seen or heard having new urgency as an offering to the beloved or gift from them.

And writing all the time of *autumn, autumn, autumn*. That

promised land where we'd find a way – *like Leonard, Trekkie, her husband Ian* – to begin *a shared life* in some unconventional shape and form.

Until then, signs and wonders. The natural world delivering us omens and auguries almost daily. Thirty thousand bees arriving in his attic so that his once-quiet rooms began making the same sound as his head, his heart: a *bloodbuzz*. Wren he found in an empty honey jar drying on a windowsill just as I'd said that I was *no, not at all*, the bright and flighty bird he imagined me from my late and strange public exhibition but only *a small brown thing*. Rare feathers – reds, blues, greens, from woodpeckers, jays that fell to my feet as never before or since. These and other phenomena which he recorded in a pocketbook as field guide to a time of marvels we believed would only repeat and increase for us yearly.

In those first weeks of love declared and returned, even the pancake batter I made early every Saturday became a wonder to me. In a kimono open to air from the back garden, I felt myself full of grace, a body and mind in balance at last. Yes, how alive those old routines were now I was cared for by a man beyond the house, for whom my every gesture was of interest. He wanted to know what I did, and how, each hour of my ordinary day. And the bread rolls I baked so often – he joked that I should bring double rations whenever we could be together: half to eat and the rest for him to preserve as artefacts, as relics. Just as he must have my hairpins to keep with him.

To have these pieces of me deemed treasure in this way was what I'd wanted through my whole lonely girlhood and it awoke in me a type of love I'd never known before. Stupidly glad and self-abasing. It would have been enough, I mean, only to travel on trains beside him, and walk through museums with my arm through his while he taught me what I didn't know. To be a housekeeper, cook and scullery maid, guarding against disruptions to his work that I admired so much. Me, who prized self-sovereignty and had fought for it, while respecting Nye's and protecting it fiercely in our children (knowing how it felt when adults trespassed on mine). Only with this man did my restraints and defences fall away so that even as he placed me on a pedestal, I wanted rather to kneel, small and servile, by his seated self.

Remember him—before the silver cord is severed, or the golden bowl is broken; before the pitcher is shattered at the spring, or the wheel broken at the well, and the dust returns to the ground it came from.

Lines from the Bible, learned without understanding for a long-ago exam. I set down my whisk and the batter to touch my throat, my heart, my stomach – the places where guilt should be but was not. Instead, I was brimming with hope, joy. I walked through those first days like a woman carrying water, going slow and steady so as not to spill a drop.

I reached for a last egg, and found it patterned as I'd never seen one before. It was his wrist, his arm – each brown mark constellated as they were on him. I could not bear for it to break, so I got a needle and went to the sink. Emptied it, gently, to keep the shell.

A Cracking Box

A CONGREGATION. How the sculptor introduced us to his works that returned after every exhibition to the former chapel in North Wales which had been his main home for the last half-century.

And as when I encountered them first – in the civic hall of my adopted town back in those shape-shifting months of new motherhood – so I arrived among them again. In an altered state.

Nye and the children took photos of me sitting amid the giant pieces before following the sculptor and his wife (both of them now my dear friends and mentors) to the guest cottage. I stayed behind, and the pictures they sent from their phones to mine? She was a stranger to me: woman with a Mona Lisa look, sitting composed in a faded grey swimsuit and long blue skirt. On her face, the ghost of a smile.

That heady scent shared by workshops and places of worship: wood, linseed, dust, damp, stone. It was all around me now, like smelling salts, so that I half hoped the sculptures would preach me a sermon. Restore me to reason. Free me from wishing for a double life.

On the back wall, high up, were words from the Psalms, painted on a golden scroll: SANCTEIDDRWYDD A WEDDAI I'TH DY. *Holiness adorns your house.* Exactly eighteen years ago, Nye and I had married in a tiny Methodist chapel that bore a similar bit of scripture.

Yes, our anniversary day come round again. How much larger our lives had become through my writing: just the year before we'd travelled to the wild woman's hospice, and this one was being spent with an older, wiser couple who – like us – had begun with very little; all the much they had now was from joint endeavour over time. Nye and I looked – from the outside – to be growing into the same good shape as them.

All those years ago, when we married, we'd said the traditional vows and meant them, even though we ourselves were not believers and had only chosen a religious service for the sake of our elders. But how moved we'd been when the first hymn began, the same one Granny Shadrick had at her wedding. 'Love Divine, All Loves Excelling'. It was the part we'd been dreading, from a fear no sound would come out from the mouths of our friends. Instead, the roof was raised by Nye's relatives and mine: chapel-goers from different countries, they sang in harmony for us, loud and sure. What marriage at its best can be: public declaration of good intent and a joining of so much more than the couple being wed.

As I walked barefoot between the vast carved shapes, just as I'd gone among our guests at the long-ago reception, I woke to the danger I was in. Nye and I had always been committed to what we called the *romance of maintenance* – a pleasure in what was slow to grow, and requiring of daily care. Whereas my attachment to this other person was fast taking on an obscure and unstable energy I'd never intended, and which threatened to break loose. As damaging to my and others' happiness, if it did, as any axe or box of matches.

§

The next day the sculptor gave us a day-long tour of the chapel and his other studios and workshops in the town. Son and daughter followed behind him, amazed, as if among zoo animals. *Two Ubus*, with their long and reaching necks. *Nine*

Cracked Balls, laughing up from the floor. *Elephant Passing the Window. Cracking Box.*

It was this, the box, that held Nye's attention. Waist height and plainer than many of the shapes around it, he came back to it again and again: slices of unseasoned wood that the sculptor had pegged together just a few years before Nye and I met. Since that time, as the oak dried, the cube had warped and then cracked, as its maker intended but couldn't control – so that it should, he told us, *defy constraint*. But Nye, when I asked him later, saw it otherwise: *The parts were free to move and yet still they held together.*

Everything about that visit to the sculptor and his wife had this same aspect of parable. A teaching, for those who would be taught.

Our last stop was in a secret location, with the sculptor driving us there before we knew it and could remember the route. We got out by a gate, disoriented, and went into the wood which holds his best-known work.

It grew already in our heads, this living sculpture, from books read and the glimpse of it that appeared nightly on one of our TV channels between each programme. *Ash Dome*, a circle of twenty-two saplings that he planted in the late 1970s, that time of political strife and ruination in the natural world. Decades before my own slow work in response to a single vandalised tree, the sculptor had begun growing these that would see another century, calling them *a long-term commitment, an act of faith*.

Slowly, slowly, using local hedging techniques, he had grafted branches one year, begun fletching in another. Cutting, bending, bandaging, until they'd become as they were now, slim dancing figures like girls around a maypole, reaching up and in towards one another.

He let the four of us stand alone in it, and I held my finger to my lips. *Listen.* To the trees with their leaves, intermingling; a steam train going by; me and my small family, still, together.

Flight Path

IN THE WEEK BEFORE I LEFT for Switzerland, I made a rare solo visit to Mother.

Summer had become a storm season that August, but she still wanted me to see some old family graves in the deep Devon farmland where she'd spent her first ten years. There was a story to tell me at every tree and hedgerow laid by her menfolk, and so we drove slowly along the narrowing roads as branches came down and water spilled from rivers into fields.

It will kill me after all, my past. What I thought as we stumbled in a high wind through the churchyard she wanted me to see.

'There.'

Three new wooden crosses with brass plaques. *Anne. Regina. Florence.* My great-granny's three spinster sisters-in-law, who'd been buried, decades ago, without headstones, as paupers. Mother had saved up to have these markers put in place.

I was touched, terribly, and then disturbed. How much of my world view had been shaped by her mournful one, despite all my lifelong attempts to get away and get free. Because although I had my degrees and a big house in another county, these hard-pressed women going back in both my bloodlines – what centrifugal force they exerted. Pulling me back and down, like rocks in my pockets. *Yes, the weight of these women.* This role I'd been given as a small girl: to be the bearer of their stories; the one who is condemned, like Echo, to listen, while remaining herself unheard. The scrolls so full of them that my own voice was crowded out.

Now, with a place at the Swiss foundation waiting for me, and only days away, how much I wanted to get free of all that history. To break my ties instead of always weaving everything into order and meaning.

'I've had too many knocks lately in a life of them. But you, Tan, must seize every opportunity.'

Mother, talking all the time I'd been sunk in thought. It was a familiar refrain. Reminding me not to waste my life, while worrying every time I told her about something as simple as walking through fields or forests alone.

I decided, suddenly, there and then, like a woodcutter before bringing down a blade, to slice through it, once and for all.

'Yes. You and Nye are always telling me I've only got one life, as if I hadn't already had several more hard lessons in that than most. But you also both attach a condition always: *Do what you like, Tan, as long as you don't hurt anyone.* But what if what I need can't be done without it? Hurting others?'

And I said that I wasn't happy in my marriage any more. That I'd listened to the story of her two mistaken ones my whole life, but needed now to speak of *mine*.

'But my dear maid, you're a mother! And that comes first. And you're so lucky to have a husband like Nye . . .'

I asked her how she could be so sure of him, on so few short visits annually, when even then he was rarely in the room with her? That I wanted to understand, please, why he was awarded so much unconditional admiration by her and others in my life, while I was judged always against harsh and exacting standards?

'Oh, you expect so much! It's always been this way for women. And do you think there's anyone, anywhere, anyway, that's like you are?'

I was sharp now, and surgical in my determination to expose

it all, the nonsense that had gone on so long between us – to have her really hear and see me.

'*People like me?* Quiet, hard-working, with a huge capacity for caregiving? Fair, logical, methodical?'

'Oh, how much you *think*, I mean. All these big words you use at us all.'

So I told her then that there *was* someone I'd met that year who might be like me, and cared for me, as I them.

How angry she was with me then.

'How could you do that to your children?'

'*You did it to me.* Father wanted to stay, but you made him go.' What I said back, sounding in control still, but full of violence, wanting everything to break and end. And for me to be struck deaf and dumb, cast out from my past and my people. Free to spend the rest of my days in a wordless present with my new-found love, writing in a quiet corner of his studio while he worked too.

Back from my difficult time with Mother, more loudly voiced opinions before I could have some quiet weeks in another country.

'Who will look after the kids when you're away?'

'I can't bear to be apart from mine for more than a night or two. A month! How will they manage? How will you?'

'Aren't you putting Nye's job at risk by needing him at home so long?'

Said not by neighbours of my mother's generation, but in the playground by women the same age and stage as me, so I accepted that I must, after all, be a monster. That for all my care of the children all these years, so that they'd never once had a nightmare, and could read at the age of four, and ran happily into every school and social situation, there must, yes, be a fault in my mechanism. Because I felt no guilt as my time away approached, only a sense that I had earned and deserved it. And that it might, too, just save the marriage, if I could find a way over there to let my other love go.

Six typed pages: the bare essentials of what I knew about our home and children that Nye did not: how and when to do nit checks and nail-cutting, uniform orders, dinner money. Phone numbers, food preferences. Handover notes he'd asked for and I was happy to provide, although the making of them showed me, once again, how unbalanced our lives had become.

And then it was the day before. A subdued afternoon in the flower gardens with Nye and the children, unsure how to be together, given how vocal everyone around us had been about the wrongness of my going.

The day itself. I arrived hours early at our nearby airport, neat and full of nervous energy. Forty-four years old. I used my fingers to count the flights I'd made out of England in my adult life. Less than ten, and none of them, till now, alone.

Just before I turned off my phone for the journey, I watched the latest television report that had been made of my work and shown across the region. My award of a foreign residency at such a prestigious institution framed in those few minutes of film as a sweet and simple fairy tale – a Cinderella scenario giving no hint of the bloodied knees and emotional toll it had cost me to hold that ground.

'A story in its own right,' the presenter said over footage of me, mild-looking, beside the pool. 'A mother of young children who took the decision to change her life.'

As if all it takes is to wake to possibility and want it.

Weather House Revisited

I HAD ARRIVED AT MY LONG-AWAITED MONTH in another
country, after almost a decade of constant caregiving. A chance
to write without compromise, but also to *rest*. With no needs to
tend except my own, I could feast on sleep at last – one day, two
– just as I'd done on Granny's lawn the first time I left a home
behind me.

Because after all my risk, here it was: the beautiful reward.
Not only international recognition, but also practical support:
meals provided, my laundry to be done by unseen hands. Still
more miraculous, *this*: Swiss chalet of my earliest childhood,
that broken barometer in which I'd invested all my longing for
peace and quiet; here it was in adult form, for my sole use.

Treehouses, they called them, the foundation who invited
me: seven cabins, each designed to a different architect's vision,
that hang on steel cables from an open concrete canopy over
a small campus at the foot of the Jura mountains. Mine was
largest, and stunning to me on arrival, as if I were a bird flown
into one of the vast, glittering windows that mirrored Mont
Blanc. *All mine?* Four open-plan floors of wood and glass, and
reached by a steep metal staircase that lifted me – so earthbound
always – clear from the ground.

I'd arrived just before a national holiday, the programme
manager explained, so that he and the other staff would be away

for my first three days. My few fellow residents were also, he thought, elsewhere that weekend.

Before dark on the first night, I was still a while simply enchanted by where I found myself, dashing up and down to photograph every exquisite fixture and fitting.

At the top of the treehouse was a picture window overlooking Lake Geneva that was twice my height and length. There, at its built-in writing ledge, I unrolled in readiness a stretch of my fifth and last scroll (twenty thousand more words to pull from memory and imagination when I'd already done four times that).

On the level below was my bed in an alcove across from a balcony that faced onto the foundation's plaza; visitors in the last light of day were pretending to try the locked door of the many-storeyed library just opposite while peering up at me and nudging one another (the treehouses had just opened so that we, their first residents, were a spectacle and source of local curiosity).

Down again was a kitchen with a massive glass wall that backed onto the mountains and their perimeter of black pines circled by birds of prey.

Then, on the lowest layer, the only space with a door I could close: a bathroom with a hard marble floor.

Which is where, despite all the rich hospitality of my hosts, I lay myself down from the small hours of the first night and then each that came after in the month I was there.

§

What's wrong? What has happened to you? Nye wanted to know, and then the other man, when I began to sob on each of their first calls to me. *I can't sleep.* I said. *Not the first night, not this last one. Not at all. I'm so frightened.*

'Well just come home,' said my new love. 'You can't stay there scared, without sleep.'

'You must tough it out,' said Nye. 'This chance won't ever come again. Work all night and nap in the days, if that's what it takes.'

What was wrong? What was happening?

Wedged between the wall and the sink, in a tangle of blankets on that bathroom floor, I suffered through those foreign nights – as I could not have foreseen – all the horrors of childhood come back. Dormant in my nerve endings and eardrums since finding Nye, they'd needed only this precise combination of fields and solitude and silence to return. It was just anxiety at first (natural perhaps for an untravelled woman alone in a new place after hardly ever a night apart from her husband) and made manifest by a repetitive checking of every cupboard, drawer and window before lying down. But then, in the early hours of my third sleepless night, the flashbacks began.

Anger, unhappiness. The terror of being behind a thin bedroom door, trying to decide if I needed to run out and put myself between her and him. Their shouting, their swearing, and the absence of sound that came after always, as if a mine shaft had collapsed – me waiting, breath held, for signs of survivors. Present again now as muffled voices, and then coming shockingly close to my ear: Mother, my stepfather, a teacher who'd refused to help when I said one day I was scared to go home. Others I didn't recognise but who also seemed real and in the room, not imagined. Faces too, less often, but right inside my shut eyes when they came. Teeth bared. Full of fury. Memories arriving, loud and uninvited. Outside my control. So many terrible old moments scraping static over my radio waves. A storm front rolling in and felt as pounds of atmospheric pressure, with only this to shelter me: cold stone walls of a small bathroom; stories my new love had recorded for me as an antidote that I played over and again for their echo. His voice becoming my lifeline so that any idea I'd brought with me of letting him go on my return? Impossible now to contemplate.

The Brute Heart

I LOVE YOU STILL and I love now someone else.

What I said to Nye halfway through my time away, when I knew I'd found at last a thing in me I couldn't bury, as I had my earliest treasures. Speaking after that first blunt admission with algebraic care and feeling the weight of every awful word as it left my mouth. Aware I might be breaking my marriage without hope of repair.

Ask me anything and I'll answer. But only once we're together, and able to see each other, and touch. He should find someone to have the children for a night and fly over, as soon as possible. The talk we needed to have should happen here, away from other people.

But there was no need for that? No problem? He'd always understood my need for close connections.

He ended the call then to resolve a dispute between our son and daughter, as I'd done so often when he tried to speak to me from his office.

My relief was instant and helium-light. The sense of my heart as a gas canister all summer, straining to contain my hazardous wants and wishes, this eased for a moment.

An out-breath.

I'd got away with it.

An in-breath, deep and unsteady.

But I didn't deserve that. Or want it.

I phoned again and we began the shortest, hardest conversation of our long marriage.

Arrivals at Geneva airport, just a day later.

Me behind the red line opening my arms to Nye's beloved body, only to find him lighter than I remembered, as if he'd made the short flight on his own, without a plane. Hollow-boned as a bird and needing me, lead-heavy with guilt, to hold him up.

How surreal, that single afternoon and night together.

To be alone of a sudden after so long with the children always near, and in a foreign country so that we looked, perversely, like newly-weds on honeymoon.

When we both began to cry on the escalator, I pulled us into a photo booth on the train station concourse, seized by magical thinking, as if conjuring – *quick* – photographic evidence of love everlasting might save us. But the machine only swallowed our money without the thing we needed from it, so that we laughed about bad omens while becoming frantic in our attempts to get something out, and using all our loose coin, until I saw there was another one at the far end of the platform. Running there then to find – *relief, reprieve* – that it worked.

Back at the treehouse, after a careful train journey turned outwards in a shared wonder at the landscape, we climbed to the top floor and sat on the long desk, facing, with feet touching. Made tiny as figures in a model railway by the giant window with its distant view of the Alps, and seeing one another outside the intimate machinery of our domestic life for the first time in a decade – that engine in which we each had our fixed, efficient parts.

His questions.

Not *when* and *where*, but *what*.

What was I thinking? What did I want? What was I trying to do?

Such restraint – this setting aside of himself when his self was so hurt – was a rare gift from a husband to wife. Allowing me for the first time, and so late, to voice something I'd always wanted, all my life, and still more since coming so close to it during my near-death.

I want peace. I said. *I'm so tired. I want to be rescued from the past by love. So much, a surfeit, given and received, every day for the rest of my life, so I forget everything that hurts. I want to slip free of self. Get lost.*

I'd tried to heal myself the slow way, I said, as the books of wisdom tell us to do. I'd placed my faith in effort and self-examination. Had dedicated myself to the making of meaning through mothering, art and service. But it was just *too hard*, and it hadn't *worked*. My life had got larger, richer, but it hadn't banished my *sadness*. And so, like a child, like an addict, I wanted now the quick fix. *Love*: if only I could get enough of it in me, around me. *Love*: the amniotic, the anaesthesia. *Love*: the drug, the cure.

Despite Nye's earlier calm and kindness, I still believed that admitting fully to my wounded self would be the end of our marriage. And yet I knew also that this triangular thing in me – there since the loss of Father, as if I were an *incomplete atom, missing an electron* – this had to be owned now and a solution sought. Even if I lost both Nye and the other man. Even at the cost of my good name. Those outcomes being less shameful to me at that moment than pretending I was made differently or better.

I waited then for Nye's anger to resound through the glass-and-steel house.

But when he spoke it was with the same care I'd used on the phone call that summoned him there.

Well, he'd always known about this side of me, and he was not a jealous man, or possessive. You couldn't read all the books we had and believe in narrow ownership of another person. And yet it was *unlikely to end well*, he suspected. So many variables branching out from this moment, few of which we could control. But his overriding hope was that I would stay with him, and not only for the sake of the children. Did I *really* still love him? He *felt* I did?

Yes. Yes. And while it was no logic that would be admitted for my defence in a court of law, I said that for me it was much like becoming the mother of one child, then two: love for my son had not (as I feared) been diminished by the unplanned arrival of his sister – and nor would anyone have thought well of me if I'd refused her for coming after him. In the same way, my heart had simply divided and enlarged that season to hold another person. And I didn't need to leave, nor want to, but neither could I walk away from that other man, however long the odds of it working out. I wanted this in the same deep-seated way he, Nye, had yearned to have children, but whereas his desire was considered natural, and reasonable, mine – I knew – was not.

And then it was morning already, with his return flight to catch.

We walked down the steep hill from the foundation through its nearby village to the little local line, just tracks in a field. Holding each other close, nose to nose and eyes closed, so that the train when it came surprised us, with me jumping on but Nye running back to fetch a forgotten bag from the grass. And as he did, the doors shut and the train moved away. I had our phones, his passport, our money; he spoke no French. Reason, when I could summon it, told me he would stay there and wait for me to get off and return. But what shook me, of course, was this too-soon and too-literal enactment of how very close we'd come to parting.

§

After all this, my last weeks in Switzerland passed in an unexpected state of quiet euphoria. The nights remained difficult, but the days were newly infused with hope. Nye back home had begun to paint and decorate for my return (wanting, he said, an immediate act to mark our new start); my other love was promising to have a writing table ready for me, while worrying that it wasn't already in place.

I was helped, too, in my final days there, to a new sense of my art and its purpose by a fellow resident, Philippe.

I'd confessed to him very early on that my act of long-distance writing had become demonic, pulling everything relentless in me to the surface so I had no illusions any more of my niceness. *Give her enough rope and she'll hang herself.* A grim phrase heard often in childhood, said by adults behind the backs of the foolhardy few who attempted anything out of the ordinary. *Give her enough rope.* My mile of words had begun as a break for freedom, a braid made of language, by which I could let myself down from the high and narrow tower of marriage and motherhood. But now it felt like a noose I'd made for my own neck, or an albatross to hang around it.

A photo shoot had been arranged by the foundation for my penultimate day, when the scroll I'd made there would be unfurled, Rapunzel-fashion, from the top floor of the library – *but after that?* I'd return to England with empty pockets and no prospects, having made a folly that would never be read, sold or exhibited.

'There's somewhere nearby you need to see,' Philippe said.

Which is how we arrived at the Collection de l'Art Brut in his home town of Lausanne, where – in its dark downstairs – he steadied himself on his crutches, and told me in his beautiful low voice that *these were my people.*

Like me, like him, the artists collected in that place made their work out of and despite their difficulties. Disenfranchised by illness, poverty, stigma, abuse or abandonment, *still they created.* And my art, like theirs, was *brut* – raw – because of its extraordinary scale and self-imposed rules to guard against annihilation. A reparative response, at the site of a wound.

'But there the resemblance ends, because we have our long educations and are able to connect with others as they could not. And your storytelling *will not end with the scrolls*, my dear, freed sister.'

Such fondness I felt then, such gratitude, for that man born with brittle bones who paid for every public event with days of pain, while laughing about being *a tiny crippled guy in a wheelchair* who was actually six foot tall if stretched flat. It was not easy for him to have brought me there so soon after an exhausting festival performance.

Philippe could no longer manage the stairs, so he sent me on alone and I went up like a novitiate: shy, serious, a little light-headed. Restored by him, and then by the collection's careful curation of those outsider artists, to a sense of my own value.

Helga Goetze. Marguerite Sirvins. Madge Gill. Ni Tanjung. I photographed their work and wrote out their biographies, moved by the forces that bore down on them – bereavement, menopause, breakdowns, imprisonment in asylums – and what they made from their rags of time and material. A wedding dress created by a woman who would never marry, crocheted from thread salvaged from old bandages. Explicit tapestries made by a middle-aged mother of seven to protest for female sexual libera-tion. Paper figures coloured and cut by an impoverished widow in a windowless room to commemorate her lost relatives.

These women and more, expanding their second half of life from scraps and fragments.

As had I, kneeling down in my forties under the weight of my longing and lostness; brought to my knees by a wish to be of use in that way of older times and places: blacksmith, hearth-tender, healer, hedge teacher. And out of that strange and stubborn want, what I'd forged was no, not folly. It was art.

§

Perhaps my private life would resolve in the same way on return to England. I'd voiced now my want for two men, a double life, and had not yet lost everything. After this, then, what?

Abundance.

Why not? It existed here, look.

My host had put her great wealth to wide and philanthropic use.

And I'd been, for just one unexpected evening, at a nearby chateau with its own richly endowed arts programme, where I was shown rooms named after the writers that were its first guests: Camus, Hemingway, Nabokov. And Philippe had introduced me there to his friend, the manager, who laughed when I stopped mid-sentence at the sight of a watercolour on the wall beside us. *Was it a Henry Miller?*

'So many visitors don't know he painted. Your face when you noticed: how lovely. Yes, you must come here to us next.'

And. And. And. Every simple thing seeming new-minted, illumined, a treasure; after so much risk and effort. I went along like a child with a basket in the woods, gathering every last sight and sensation. Free-wheeling on a borrowed bike past log piles, pines; filling my headscarf with walnuts from the village tree; feeding sparrows on a blue tin table; smiling at a farmer who sang to his cows, then me.

Then it was there. My last day. Eyes full of Alps. Feet in Lake Geneva.

My feet in Lake Geneva!

And my heart began to beat then like a big and bloody drum.

I'd worked so hard for this. To reach beyond the edge of town and convention together. But what were the chances? Of having at last these two men to compensate for the one I was without when growing? More used to ashes, I dared then at the water's edge to count my coin.

My husband loved me. *He* loved me.

How well I would care for them both!

And I whispered it, despite the risk of tempting fate.

Right there, right then. I had all I ever wanted.

LIMBO

shape-shifting

What is a man anyhow?
What am I? What are you?

Enigma of Arrival

HUSBAND.

I came home from Switzerland to a man transformed. As I'd been in the weeks before the birth of our children, driven by a tireless wish for a clean nest, so Nye was now.

Since his visit to me, his eyes were opened, he said. He'd been jealous of my life moving on, he saw now, while his felt fixed until retirement. And he'd lost his inner life, once so rich, through telling himself there was no room for one now he was a father and bread-winner, whereas the truth was more difficult to admit: he'd become lazy – it was too easy to get pleasantly numb from a beer on the train, computer games, television. That burst of creative endeavour we'd enjoyed in our twenties, and which I'd summoned again in the last few years – it took persistence in the face of few rewards, and he'd become used to a monthly salary that compensated him so well for his effort. But he'd bought, look, a notebook for the flight home and was writing again, first time in years.

And it was time, he saw, to find a form of words for the children so they could understand that my childhood had been different to his and theirs. He was sorry he'd always insisted before on my saying nothing about it, so that all the stories and customs of how things were done had come from his side. We'd build, the four of us, together, a new language for family life that made more room for me to enter.

Talking about the other person in my life, we approached with caution however. Like villagers returning home after an occupation, we went through our days more gently than before in case we touched on things that were mined, explosive. So easy to say too much, and enjoy brief catharsis but a long regret, we agreed. And so we adopted instead an almost monastic silence, using smiles and small touches.

Among Nye's many, continuing kindnesses at this fragile time were a refusal to shame or blame, and a scrupulous restraint from asking questions that would drive me to confess painful details or lie about them. Mine to him were wordless acts of service. His hair, which I'd always done in a rough and impatient way, I cut with new reverence, offering always before he asked. Cups of tea, baths drawn, clothes warmed and laid out for him to find on returning from work in the rain. Little, daily ways of saying *thank you for staying / thank you for letting me.*

§

The other man.

Bird-shaped couple on the willow-pattern plate of my childhood who were always and never flying free. How it was with him and me in that autumn we'd imagined all summer: tears and laughter endlessly repeating, like an oriental scroll painting that unrolls with only an illusion of movement. No clear route forward we could find, though we tried and tried.

As on a day of many such days, when we walked together through parkland, a few feet apart, looking perhaps like a couple meeting on neutral ground after divorce. Bewildered, both, by what was being exposed in us as we tried to devise a shared life – fear, jealousy – so that we'd begun, less than a month from my return, to shrink and pull apart: creatures on an upturned rock.

And how hard it was to follow his meaning as we went, mapless, along the paths. I didn't *need* him enough. I was so *quick*, so *competent*. Too far ahead of him in thought and vision; he couldn't keep up. And what was it, again, he could give to me? He had felt, in our first weeks of working together, my great and many responsibilities, the number of people I supported – children, friends, neighbours – believing he, with his quieter life, could be that for me in turn. But I seemed now, after my time away, so *vivid*, so *self-sufficient* . . .

Trailing behind him, hiding tears, I looked for trees I knew and said their names to keep myself upright as they were. *Oak. Ash. Walnut.*

Please. I said. *Can we just sit and be quiet?*

Goldcrest. Treecreeper. Dunnock. We took a bench by a ravine of Himalayan birch and they came and came. Small birds, so many, so close, and he named them for me, sketching their shapes in the air, as if he was the first man, and that was our Eden. I wanted to explain how I'd only been made so bright from all *this* – how illuminated the world was for me in his company – but kept a hand at my mouth, trying to make myself as small and brown as the birds around us.

Hurrying away then to return me in time for the afternoon school run (meridian line that divided my fledgling double life), we climbed up through yew roots that had spread like dead men's fingers over their black stone embankment, and I saw that it was an underworld I'd joined him in. He was a lover of shadows, not light, and his life a carefully constructed labyrinth (what he'd warned me from the start, while I – silly goose – just laughed: *But I was so at home outside! All he needed to do was take my hand and join me in the fields, the beaches.*).

I dared myself to look back. Lose him, let go.

Pale sun through thinning trees. His dear solid shape. *No, I couldn't bear it. To be without him.* Hands became fists in my pockets, holding tight to my idea of a right-shaped life. As if I alone, through force of want and will, could bring the three of us into the neat geometry I needed, and then keep us there.

He'd given me keys to his workshop to use on my return, but the long days of shared projects I'd dreamed of enjoying there were happening only rarely. More times, I'd arrive, smiling, at the agreed time and date, to find him unwell and distracted by something in the larger part of his life that was closed to me. And for all my skill at paying close attention to the needs of other people, *I couldn't follow him.* His talk as a maze of unfinished sentences, full of subjunctives, conditionals – *if, then, when* – so that I'd become too cheerful, or impatient, then desperate in my attempts to return us to the bright and simple possibilities of *here, now, together.*

I had believed until then that love, when reciprocated, formed an instant trinity with clarity and trust, this being the experience of my quick-made yet enduring bond with Nye. But I was learning now a very different version, one in which a notebook was filling with diagrams, lists and equations made by an engineer straining to design a future which could contain me and everything else he wished to keep safe. I, with my farming heritage, was prepared to bear many seasons of trial and discomfort in the hope of one day achieving *abundance, increase*; he, meanwhile, had begun to speak of *tension, shearing, torsion, fatigue.*

Alone there one cold day, I knelt to the old stove that was hard to keep going. Trying to tend it as Granny had her fire, always fond, slightly girlish, as if wooing it.

That same patient way she and other country folk would hold out handfuls of hay to an animal, or crusts for a garden bird, hoping for it to come; enjoying the slow and uncertain kindling of interest: how it was to care for that man who was finding it hard to decide his life.

I felt in the scuttle for the smallest bits of coal to sprinkle onto the sticks I'd lit, taking care not to overwhelm the wood that was still catching. *Why could I not find the same restraint and pace with him? Forget all the heady shared visions we'd conjured in words that summer, and see what steadier pleasures might be settled upon? Yes, I must learn to hold back instead of being this fool rushing in.*

Putting my hands to my nose, I snuffed at the smoke on my fingertips. Smiled at what we'd been talking about over the phone earlier. *Coal tar. What was it really? Why was it used to clean and cure?* We'd been swapping memories of our childhood sick days, from being so ill always that autumn (as if even our immune systems were reluctant for us to become close). The bread poultices my mother made me wrap around bad throats; how his gave him crushed aspirin in a spoonful of malt extract.

Oh how old we both were. What I understood, all of a sudden, eyes stinging. Smoke. Longing. Loss. *More past time spent apart than we could have as shared future.*

Slow Time of Accidents

SORDID.

The children were at the breakfast table, dressed for school, eating the bread rolls I'd risen at five to make ready for them. Our two cats were by their food bowls. I could hear a magpie outside. Cups and plates were stacked unbroken in the cupboards. Yes. Everything that was there in the minutes before I read the letter, was there still. Intact.

Sordid.

I saw the envelope as it came through the door, too early for the postman, and I went to greet whoever had hand-delivered it, but they'd somehow hurried already out of sight.

I recognised the writing then and wondered why this dear friend had put a note through the door instead of knocking or calling. It was the woman I'd met in the park so long ago, who had been ever since a daily and loving presence in my children's lives. I had a key to her house, and she mine. Whenever she was ill, I brought her supplies; she did the same for me. And we had, despite our great difference in age, a shared appetite for fun, and a gift for making it from the simplest materials: even spring-cleaning the house could have us doubled up with laughter.

Sordid.

How she ended our friendship, there and then, with that letter landed on my doormat. Without knowing the details, or asking for them, she had learned (how, I would never know) that I cared now for another man. This, to her, long-widowed of her beloved husband, was unforgiveable. She would have nothing more to do with me.

Who could blame her?

I'd have liked the chance to explain, to tell her that Nye knew, that we were attempting something honest, but then again, I'd done it, hadn't I? Gone beyond the pale. Outside of what was normal in my time and place. And I'd *wanted* this: to know how it would be to get free of playing safe, craving approval. Being bounded by the good opinion of others.

Now I'd found out, and it was awful.

The letter happened in early November, just a month after my return from Switzerland, and I stopped eating soon afterwards. If things had been more secure with that other man, I might have recovered from the shock and shame of it, but he – after receiving a similar note from someone likewise close to him – had retreated into silence.

As I'd been as a very small girl, stricken by Father moving beyond my reach, so I was again. I felt hungry for a while, then I didn't. Had thirst but the effort involved in boiling a kettle or filling a glass from the tap meant I postponed it for hours at a time. Going to the toilet, the same: there was an ache some-where down there, but dull, and distant.

In this way, slowly, slowly, and without any outward signs at first, I began to let go of living. A water infection soon set in and deepened, spread. All the symptoms from the previous year's end that had been so mysterious, coming back – but familiar now, like friends. I knew what might happen to my lungs and my kidneys if I simply left myself untreated.

Meanwhile, my late-made public self – which I'd assumed would be put away with the last word on the final scroll in Switzerland – had begun to take on a life of its own, and earn money. Would I guest tutor on a creative writing course? Come to Broadcasting House to record a programme for the BBC? Consider an art installation in Covent Garden? Come for final discussions about a residency in a university library, now funding was approved? Travel north to tell the wild woman's story to an audience of several hundred? *Yes*, I said, *yes*, even as the effort of getting to and from these places had me collapsing on station platforms, falling down stairs.

'*In Tanya's words one can feel the sense of personal ownership and self-sufficiency . . . Nobody rules you, nothing has ruined you, you are gleefully, determinedly, yourself.*' Written about me in a book that had just come out from an author who'd visited me at the swimming pool in my first summer there. Now, as we met again, only a year later, sharing a stage at a big speaking event in the Lake District, I was glad we didn't have much chance to talk. She was still as I remembered her – funny, clever, strong – while I'd fallen very far from what it was she'd seen in me and praised.

§

Just before Christmas, I let myself into that bower on the Downs I'd first stepped into at the year's start, a stranger on work business.

I'd always feared what would break loose in me if I ever one day showed my real and raw needs, and now I knew. I'd become disruptive of my peace and his. Disgusting to myself and others. Yes, what a mad and self-harming attachment I had now to the man who worked there, to be thinking always of what I'd sacrifice. *As in*: what I wouldn't give – *my hair, a foot, a finger* – to have him back as he was first to me. As if anyone wants their beloved with shorn hair and missing limbs, wearing sackcloth and ashes. Abject. Pitiful.

I am become a charnel house. Phrase said always now at the end of my dreams that were all nightmares, in which my phone was broken, and my car was broken, and my legs, so I could not reach him, and could not reach him, and could not reach him.

Uncanny, to hear in sleep that word, *charnel*, which I had to look up on waking the first time, only to find it confirmed my sense of dismemberment. A chamber strewn with bodies come apart.

But those rooms around me, in that last time I'd be there alone? They were dear to me as always, from being his.

The sounds of them: orchard ducks, chimney pigeon, distant train. And the smell, composed of all good things: soap, metal shavings, wood glue, solder, him.

Never able to have us close and in the open as I wanted, this is how I'd ended up loving him instead: *in pieces, through pieces, to pieces*. And he was my match in that, caring for me best when he could apprehend me in parts, from a distance. Collectors, both of us: archiving always as insurance against loss, even while it was this behaviour that caused the breakage.

Terrible clarity about that during my slow movement through those rooms I'd soon be without. As I'd been during my last minutes alone in Granny's home after sending her away to hospital, gathering up every obsolete appliance as keepsake – I'd been doing it again, with him. In a trunk under a bed at home, I had things of his he'd given me: an old blue shirt, a shaving brush, a sketchbook. While here, in his studio, were my hair-pins in a pot. A torn headscarf. Books of mine with passages I'd underlined, which he loved, he said, because he could use them to follow my mind in its movements.

So few material proofs of my life in his.

I sat at his workbench for a while, the radio on, summoning the nerve to go for good. Joni Mitchell, singing about reindeers, trees, a river.

When the song ended, I put my key down and left, closing the door behind me. The worst hurt of my young years – my father's house, inaccessible – I inflicted now on myself, as a woman.

§

Back home, in what was now my only set of rooms again, I conducted the business of Christmas, while a noise like wrapping paper began to crackle in my chest. As with the near-death, I could feel myself going *away away*. Not so fast this time, or so painless, but the same pull and siren call. Little boat, big ocean. Not much longer left to suffer. I tried to care about the people I'd be leaving, but I had reached the end of empathy and strength. I wanted only for my own hurt to end.

And then it was somehow New Year's Day, and Nye saying I maybe needed fresh air, even though it was so wild and windy? We drove to the nearby sea along roads I'd last travelled with the other man in autumn; the rivers had burst their banks so that fields I'd walked in with him were underwater now. *Pheasant*, I said in my head, seeing one. *Heron. Steeple.* As if noticing and naming things would keep me from slipping away. Posts to tie my rope around.

We parked, and buttoned our big coats against the cold, before walking along the seafront in a gale. Me, Nye and our daughter. When we reached the Martello tower at the far end, it was clear I couldn't breathe properly and so Nye said he would go back for the car and bring it to me there. I wanted to be alone then, stricken as I was, but my girl said no, she wouldn't go with Dad, she'd stay with me. I could hear her beside me, and see her too, in my peripheral vision.

Rook. I said to myself, trying to stay upright. *Jackdaw.*

Went then to take my daughter by her ungloved hands, and pull her close, face to face, so we could share the warm pockets of my tweed coat.

She was gone.

Shouting her name into the high wind, I ran around the low circular wall of the tower's deep and dry moat, one way, then the other, to look along the empty beach, left and right. Ran next into the nearby toilet block with its heavy metal doors and wet concrete floor. Began after that to look into the parked cars, and ran then in front of one that was pulling out, driven by a man on his own, that had, when I looked, a bundle in the back seat, under a blanket. I yanked the door open, yelling, as the man shouted back about phoning the police.

Knew then there was only one place left she could be. Fifty feet below, on the hard tarmac of the tower's sunk foundations. As I had fallen from a wall at that age, during a disaster in my mother's life, so now I – neglectful, undeserving – had lost my precious daughter.

Nye and our car returned then, pulling in beside me. And in that minute that took forever, I became a woman whose daughter was dead, or dying, or disappeared. And nothing in the lives of Nye or my son or me would ever be right or whole again without her, and it was my fault.

What's wrong? What's happened to you? Nye got out, engine still running, and grabbed hold of me, listening. *No. No. She ran to catch me up, Tan. She's in the back of the car, strapped in, look.*

She was. And how, I will never know. I go back there sometimes and walk it, like a coroner. I've made a diagram. Nothing explains it, other than the awful possibility that I was, for a few minutes, *out of my mind* with sickness and sorrow. Not for long, but time enough to lose a child.

I want to say this was the end of my dangerous behaviour. That I came to my senses, at once and forever. That the month spent in bed after that with pneumonia was a time of recovering my reason and self-respect along with my health. I want to say that when I was next able to dress and drive – with everything still hurting – I did not begin to meet that man again, on the still more diminished terms he offered. But I did.

So quick to learn, all my life, in everything, I was slow and stupid in this.

Last Words

WAS THERE ANY PATIENCE LEFT IN ME? *Could we meet? I should say when and where.*

What that man asked of me at the end of March, after our new year's attempt at a once-weekly arrangement had already foundered into hurt and confusion.

And because I guessed now it would always be this way with him – these tidal comings and goings of closeness, like caring for a deep-sea fisherman or an oil-rig worker – not ever in my control, I mean, and yet bearable, just, for the pleasure of his company when he was back on land and happy – because of this, I said where, and when: *Tomorrow, by the church, in sun.* But he'd made a mistake with his dates, and so we met instead the day after, in rain.

When I returned home, hours later, heavy with weather and tears, there were three messages.

From London, a letter congratulating me on being accepted as a Fellow of the Royal Society of Arts, with the freedom of their fine Enlightenment-era building in the heart of that city I'd fled from in my twenties.

From my mother, a voicemail. My father had died that afternoon following a year or more of cancer treatment. Someone in town had stopped her to say. As far as she knew, he'd left no word for me, nor should I expect one from the family he made after us.

From my love, a text. Sent while I was heading home and away from him. Thanking me for offering everything I had, making room, changing things. Meeting again, when he asked. But I was always looking over my shoulder back down the hill at him, pointing at the highlands I saw over the ridge. He had tried to keep up but I walked too fast, and he carried too much weight.

The anguish of earliest childhood returning in full force at all this, so I dropped to the floor, where Nye found me hours later. Broken – too soon after my last mending – by that wild shifting of size and shape in which, despite my lifelong attempts to fix myself, I was – *yet again, and all at once* – deemed *special, too much and nothing.*

What we have waited for too long, or possessed only in secret, or had for too short a while: how hard it is to walk through our days with a loss not apparent. To have survived endings that had no ceremony and called forth no condolences. That were bereft even of a grave or death certificate. Sadness without sign or symbol.

On the day of my father's funeral, I sat in a car above my childhood beach, back to the land. Willing myself to stay put until the service was over and the mourners dispersed. Only at evening would I dare to drive to the town square of my first twenty years just to stand unseen for a minute. Not in remembrance, but defiance.

It's me. I'm here. This was my town too.

But before that, grief work. A grim alternative eulogy for the man being buried without me, said aloud to the sand, the sky and birds: the natural world which had always been a more reliable source of comfort.

THE LAST TIME I HEARD FROM MY FATHER

I was thirty, back at work after putting Granny away. The phone went and I answered, absent-minded. Someone asking for me by the married name I never used. *Who is this?*

Him.

Clearing his throat, hesitating a moment, before saying I earned more than he did, and since I'd had his mother put away, he was spending a lot on petrol for visits. *You want me to give you money?* My voice hard, though my legs gave way. *How much?* Fifty a month would cover it. (The first secret I ever kept from my husband, so ashamed was I to be paying the man who'd abandoned me.)

THE LAST TIME I SAW MY FATHER

A year after the birth, the haemorrhage, the inheritance. Sitting with Nye, my mother, my stepfather and baby son in a strip-lit garden centre on a visit home. *How are you, Mar?* A man saying hello before seeing who Mother had with her. Food stopping in my mouth.

Him.

He realised my presence and refused it in a moment that unfolded in slow motion. Not even having the grace to turn and go, but continuing to the counter, choosing food. Me looking at the rest of my too-small family and asking why they were silent at this offence. What spell of cowardice or convention had them keep their seats? I ran to the toilets then and wept, before deciding to go in and confront him myself. *Here is your grandson. I am your daughter.* But he had used my leaving to leave himself. His meal left untouched on the table.

Now, on the clifftop, I had in my pocket the single silver cufflink I'd kept back on the day in early childhood when I interred in the garden fragments of Father's left-behind life.

I was done now with loving like this. Treating the least little thing from impossible men as holy relics.

He was no god, and only ever out of reach for me, remember. For balance, for fairness, I dared myself then to admit the good in him. How close he and my half-brother were, so that they'd worked together in the same garage for years. The care with which he'd tended Granny's bungalow and back garden decade after decade, even while she continued deaf to him and loud in praise of his older brother. His beautiful singing voice – only thing I'd inherited from him, and in a diminished form, but enough to delight my son and daughter at bedtime.

That would do.

I placed the cufflink on a patch of bare earth in the thin grass of the clifftop and drove inland to my old home town.

'You! Come here, come in, I've got something to show you.'

This being said to me the minute I stepped out from my car. It was my first employer, café owner, coming out for air and speaking to me as if my last shift had been a day ago, not decades.

(*How known I was still, how familiar my face, after so much time away!*) 'You know your father was buried today, I suppose?'

I nodded. Followed him past chairs and tables I'd wiped a thousand, thousand times in my teens, to the kitchens at the back.

'Have you seen the death notice though?' He began to go through old newspapers used to wrap the chips (how I'd learned about books before I had many, reading reviews from the broadsheets' culture supplements between customers).

'There, read that.'

Him.

Disappointed at my sharp hunger to see, at least, my name in print beside his in the obituary, I scanned fast, back turned. *Passed peacefully away . . . Special and beloved husband . . . Much loved dad . . . Loving grampy . . .* I counted how much larger his second family. His wife, my half-brother, two stepchildren, eight grandchildren. *But me, his firstborn? And my son, my daughter?* Absent from the record.

'And have you looked at this week's yet?' Before I could arrange my face, he opened the latest edition.

Me.

FORMER STUDENT RECEIVES ROYAL SOCIETY OF ARTS HONOUR.

A half-page feature, using information I'd given a local journalist just weeks before my father's death, but published only now – by chance, not design – in the week of his funeral.

'Got the last word, didn't you, Tan?' Said Mother, later, when I told the tale.

No, I thought. *He did.*

A week later, a postcard arrived for me. A bright, outdated photo of the place I'd just returned from, with this on the reverse: *The town is proud of you.*

Sent by my first teacher (in her late eighties now), the one who'd advised me when I was just five to get *away away* from there to university. And it wasn't much, but neither was it nothing, her gesture. It felt precious to me then, poor as I was in family. To be told I was remembered and that my name meant something good back there.

Shape-shifting

FROM EASTER, AFTER MY LOSS OF LOVE and Father's funeral, I simply climbed inside the wild woman's diaries and hid there. Without a purpose or identity of my own any more, and with no place I needed to be, I took her days for my own. The time had come to make the book I'd promised her.

I worked night and day after that, stopping only when the children needed me or tears in my private hours blurred my sight too much to see the pages I was proofing.

How fiercely alive she is at fifty, after her mastectomy. Always *striking out, forging through, plunging head first.* She teeters, she clambers, she sinks, shouts and laughs. With her many friends, she shoots down rapids, is drenched by cascades, swims in snow and rain, skinny-dips under full moons and floats down fast estuary tides, umbrella aloft and flower garland in her hair.

And the landscape matches her appetite for it, delivering great big portions of nature that are food to her, and drink. Rivers foam like beer, or go thick and rich in her hands as ginger cake made with black treacle. Waters that run gin-clear one month are dark as stewed tea the next.

Nothing on her Dartmoor goes unnoticed, unnamed, unloved. The last of a season's crab apples are celebrated as *fruity tiara on a tipsy granny at a barn dance* and even horse dung is described as a delicacy for her dog.

The music of the river fades as we walk away. As she felt upon leaving the festival that every swim after cancer represented, so I felt each time I emerged from the vivid present tense of her writing.

But the contrast between us – she all brown, bruised and full of muscle; me become so soft – was painful: two years of kidney and chest infections had left me with a fear of cold water, so that I was bereft of my old and enlivening swimming rhythms. I spent most of that hot summer in jeans and thick woollens, hiding from my body as well as life.

§

'*The strange angel!* Hello again. What are you doing here in the shadows?'

It was June now and pool season again, but instead of being centre stage as I'd been the last two years, I was back to my old role of minding children's clothes, while also now trying to proofread. There was just a month until the wild woman's book went to print, so it could be launched in September at a big outdoor swimming event where hundreds would celebrate her life and legacy.

The man who'd come to sit beside me was how I remembered him from our first and only meeting the summer before, when we'd enjoyed hours of talk like bread, wine: fully shared and generous. And perhaps it was that – the memory of that fine exchange – and the fact of his being separate to all my circles of belonging, that made me feel able to say the truth. That I'd made a great mistake in my life around the time he and I first met, getting lost in a situation I couldn't understand until I'd been hurt beyond the point of endurance, recovery. That once the book I was making for a dead woman was done, then I was finished too. I'd keep going for my husband and children of course, but for myself? I was empty of hope.

Did I remember what he'd said at our last meeting? About the old house in Devon he'd taken on from a distant relative? That was my birth county, yes?

I nodded. Yes and yes. Though he hadn't told me where it was down there?

When he said the name of the tiny village, every hair on my arms went up, despite my jumper. A quiver of many little antennae. Because the place he was restoring in deep, deep country was only a mile, less, from the gateways where my granny and grandad went courting.

He needed to make a trip to it soon. Would I like to be his driver up and back, and use the house to complete my commitment to this other woman? I'd given him a gift of conversation the previous year, back when he was newly arrived in England after decades abroad – I'd seemed then a blessing on his return. His house might now be that for me?

And so it came to pass that I finished the wild woman's book in a place reached through the lanes where Granny Shadrick had grown up. The smells, the hedgerows, the breed of cows in the fields – all a balm to my sore soul, even before we arrived at the cottage composed of fairy-tale elements. Buddleias and brambles pressed against the windows, swifts flew out from the eaves, and bees from the brickwork – everything humming with light and life.

That night, once dark came, with a fire in the grate and candles to see by, I got to work. Not, that first evening, on the book. I'd also brought with me a blanket I'd begun to crochet the day after my other love had decided against a shared life. Fingers teaching heart to hold fast, as during infertility and the time of Granny's dying.

Twisting the wool in and out, and smiling as my new friend told tales from countries far away, I shared then some of my humbler ones from places close to the house.

'This is how you'll write a book of your own, you know.'

'How so?' I stopped working to look across at him.

'Like that.' He mimed some invisible knitting. 'You're exhausted now. Believe yourself finished. But you've got so much to say. You just need the right theme or question to pull it all up and into shape.'

A log didn't tip then, burning, from the fire to the old brown carpet. Brambles didn't tap the glass. Wind didn't roar in the chimney. We continued talking as before. But inside me, something shifted.

I began to apprehend again my own strength. I'd never be a wild woman swimming; I wasn't built for rivers, any more than I was suited to wielding chainsaws like the sculptor. I was more like the wood and water itself. Slow growing. Slow burning. Able to dam and then channel myself into whatever I determined to do.

Space Oddity

I CAME INTO THE VILLAGE ON FOOT and alone in the late afternoon of a hot August day, with my rucksack and two straw hand baskets loaded with supplies for the tiny cliff-side cabin – belonging to the National Trust and kept closed most of each year – that was mine for the week. Camping stove, candles, large flask, little kettle, tin mugs, eggs, nuts, oatcakes – and as many copies as I could carry of *Wild Woman Swimming: A Journal of West Country Waters*, first and likely only book from the Selkie Press I'd created just for that purpose.

The next settlement along on that part of the North Devon coast was still the busy tourist destination it had been in my childhood, but here there were no pubs, no cafés, no public toilets. Nor any racks of postcards or plastic beach toys. There was, I'd been told when asking what to pack, just one cottage with a serving hatch sometimes open for hot drinks and ice cream. And the only advertised attraction for the seven days I'd be in residence, aside from the ever-present beach and sea? *That would be me.*

This had become a particular thrill in the three years of my new life as a travelling speaker and self-declared *writer of the outside*: coming alone and unknown to a place, senses made sharp by newness. Stranger in a strange land, I went along hungry for any small signs of who I'd be among this time.

But in the quarter-hour it took me to get from the car park to my cabin, I didn't see a soul. Which made it all the more peculiar to reach the little brick building I'd be in, windowless on its wall that bordered the slipway, and see on its green wooden door my own name and photo. And vertiginous to open next the smaller side entrance by the cliff edge only to find a postcard waiting for me on the cold stone floor. Sent from across that North Atlantic I'd just arrived beside by the man who wouldn't, after all, be growing old with me.

Heart lift at first, seeing his handwriting. Then heaviness. A fatigue so great that I wanted to lie on the grass and sleep, all my bags left unpacked around me. I'd come all this way, trying to keep moving through these months of mine that would always be without his company now – but here he was, ahead of me. Marking the territory.

Holding the postcard by one corner, mouse by its tail, I took it to the small outhouse that would be my only source of cold water. Came back then to the threshold to begin again, freed of male influence: a woman writer being allowed to work inside the carefully kept and Grade II-listed studio of two long-gone women artists who'd defied convention to live and love together.

Curator-cautious, I went step by step through the tiny space so as not to break anything. There on the back of the staircase door were the couple's two painting smocks, one inside the other. Hung about on hooks were their cups, a rusted nutmeg grater, a Festival of Britain jug. Then, going up the few wooden steps, and bending my head to get around the sharp turn and low ceiling, I came into their only other room. Metal-framed bed with a white counterpane, a pitcher and bowl for washing, open cupboard of art supplies. On the mantelpiece, a sinister mercury mirror I'd been warned about on the risk assessment: it was degrading fast and giving off poison – I mustn't get too close or look into its dark, decaying surface.

And so of course I did.

I'd been ashamed of my face since my terrible mistake in love: all the beauty I'd felt to possess in the few months of being wanted twice over – this had left me now. My skin was bad, my eyes were tired.

But I was here to welcome people in. What I looked like didn't matter.

I adjusted my headscarf, tightened my apron and went back down to make a little bower of books by the open door. Hoping, in this way, to recover some of the joy I'd had in my first year of writing beside the pool.

§

Remote as I was that week, confined to a few square feet of cliff edge, I felt myself connected in a new and rich way to the world: messages of congratulations kept reaching me in bursts through my wavering phone signal – the wild woman's book was arriving with those who'd pre-ordered it, several hundred people, so that the financial risk I'd taken to print it was already more than covered. *To be read outside – may it go waterlogged, sun-buckled and wind-chapped*: what I'd written as epitaph and instruction, and readers had begun to do, photographing it by water as far afield as the Arctic Circle, Australia and Canada.

And the few dozen I'd brought with me only for display, to show the kind of work I did, these too began to be picked up and examined. Every time someone asked about the book and I'd explained its unusual story, that person would insist on buying a copy. To see the diaries moving out into the world through and beyond me in this immediate way – it was a powerful magic and restored just a little of the self-respect I'd lost through my desperate behaviour in the last year.

It also concentrated my mind and courage, even while I continued to mourn my impossible love. Because good as it was to see the wild woman's words reaching people, I was sharply aware that she herself would never get to read them aloud or learn of their impact. And while I'd get to enjoy all that on her behalf . . . *it wasn't enough.* I wanted my own stories to connect me to others in that wide and deep way only books and songs ever can.

You want this, then? Even more than that man?

(My better self testing its shadow one.)

I want both, of course. Him, a book.

But. If you can only have one?

Then I choose: book.

Soul smiled, not fooled. I didn't mean it yet, but if I asked myself enough and kept saying the right thing? Hope for me yet.

§

At the end of my residency, when I was heading from Devon to Wales to collect the children from their grandparents, I got goosebumps at the song come on the radio.

Space Oddity.

Two years ago, in that other August, I'd had a night without sleep because of it. I'd gone to bed early in readiness for the five a.m. start I'd need to make for the West Country: the date made for my second visit to the wild woman. But hour after hour, I'd lain awake in the dark while just a few bits of that song played again and again in my head until – at around three in the morning – it stopped and something like a cable snapped inside me. And then an accelerating sensation straight afterwards, as if a lift was plummeting fast down its shaft towards a basement. I'd sat straight up then, gasping, hands on heart.

'She's gone, I'm sure of it.' I told Nye, having woken him with my sudden movement.

And at eleven that day, when we were already halfway to Devon, a message came through from the woman who'd greeted me on my first visit to the hospice. It wouldn't be public knowledge for a while yet but, yes, our friend had died in the night.

Now, after a week in which her book had begun to sell so

many copies before launch that I'd need already to reprint it, here it was again, that song.

I began to sing along, but part way through – it stopped. There was no static on the radio to explain the break in sound. I looked around for other cars, unnerved. None behind, or in front, or on the opposite carriageway.

Fear made a metal taste in my mouth: had I myself just died somehow? In a crash so fast and unseen by me that my mind was thrown clean of its body?

A few more awful, empty seconds of no sound other than the car's engine.

Then the music came back on and the song continued towards its usual end. I held tight to the steering wheel, telling myself to pull in carefully at the next service station. I must be more exhausted than I knew. But when the last notes were over, the presenter said it was a rare version made by Bowie with that deliberate break in it, and played now on radio for the first time.

Lifelong disbeliever in fate and design, I parked on the hard shoulder and cried and cried and cried. It would be weeks still before I'd read from the book to a packed room near to its author's beloved Dart river, with her family and many friends in attendance. And that would be a privilege, but it was also a burden. I'd been worried all summer about making the book right, and beautiful, and handling all the many arrangements needed for the launch: these practical things even small publishers have several staff to manage.

Now, as I wept by the side of the road, I felt she had found a way to send me a message. Ease the load. There was more work to do, *so much*, but in essence, it was done, wasn't it? A full two years after our only meeting, I'd kept the promise I made to her that day.

THIRD AGE

after all

Whoever you are, come forth! . . .
You must not stay sleeping and dallying
there in the house, though you built it . . .

Out of the dark confinement!

HOW TO LIVE. HOW TO DIE. How to reach back with under-standing, even as we are going beyond the ones we love.

What I wanted to learn, fast, in what I believed was my last minute of living, in that moment before I was laid awake on the operating table – these are the questions I will pursue now to my end of days. What started with an emergency having become my passion and my purpose.

In my first life, I placed my faith in rigid routines, believing I could put to sleep my wilder desires.

In my second, I went without rest, searching always for ways to escape my self and the pain of living. To slip my skin and merge, forever, with something beyond me. I tried mothering, unpaid acts of service, immersion in cold water, the making of art, and then – lastly, disastrously – I hoped to get lost in love.

After such knowledge, what forgiveness?

Think neither fear nor courage saves us.

I would meet you upon this honestly.

Fragments from Eliot. So many lines by him and other poets that I've committed to heart over the years, through fear, for courage. As if by stitching enough fine minds together, I could make of them a mantle to wrap around me. My own self, for too long, felt only as an old donkey skin I wanted to throw off, however many photographs and films were made of me, shining bright at my late-made outsider's art.

We live in only one time and place.

What a counsellor said to me at a first and only session booked too soon after the birth and its aftermath.

We live in only one time and place.

He was trying, I think, to return me briskly to reason, as if my soul was a bone to be reset. He meant it to be healing, I'm sure, but it felt, when he said it, like an excommunication. As if I was, as I feared, cast out on a lonely planet, without hope of escape or redemption. The life I woke to after that surgery was so white and cold and difficult – I needed to believe I could get free of it, somehow.

And yes, we do only have one life, so far as science and our registers of births and deaths go. It is lived in places, to clock time or the sun and its seasons. And we live in bodies, with economic and political forces bearing down on us, always. No amount of self-sacrifice or selfishness lifts us completely clear. We are not, in this world, ever really free spirits.

But to keep living in it? Sometimes we have to see our worst hurts as little deaths, and believe in our ability to be reborn by them.

Two Views of Mount Caburn

'BURIED OR CREMATED?'

A new year, and me arrived at it formless now I no longer had the wild woman's life to give shape to my own.

And whatever might be the right way to recover from the erosion of self got from giving away so much to another person: this wasn't it. Because there I was with that man again.

Yes, there we were, he and I, going among old headstones degraded with age.

There we were, despite my attempts to break the string in me he could always pull on, lightly, so that we'd continued to exchange messages (and even meet sometimes) since that March afternoon the year before when he decided not to change his life for me.

I sighed, looked around and away from him.

We were standing between graves in a churchyard that had only a low flint wall separating it from Virginia Woolf's writing shed and Leonard's precious garden. And it was his life, not hers – those years he'd enjoyed with Trekkie after Virginia's death – that we'd been more interested in. This nearby proof that such a way of life was possible – a woman dividing her time between two men – we'd supposed in our first and only summer there was an outside chance we might manage it too: be close to one another without destroying the life I'd built with Nye and the children.

But for him, it was enough now, this ghostly association. And he wasn't being cruel to me or manipulative, simply acting in the only way he could for his own soul's sake – its need for walls and locked doors, and a borderland beyond. A wonder I'd ever been let in at all.

'Buried or cremated?'

He asked me again, and I looked back at him, shrugged. Tired now of our terminal talks when at the start I'd hoped there'd be years for us to go on long walks, arm in arm and laughing, over the Downs.

'A grave, I suppose, if Firle church will take me, though I've no family in the ground there. Otherwise? Burnt, perhaps, then scattered on the Beacon.'

He looked at his phone. Time to go, again, as always. We turned away and there it was.

Mount Caburn.

Trekkie's painting, exactly. Which we'd stood beside, back in the time when we were still polite new acquaintances who hadn't hurt each other yet.

'*Of course,*' he said, into the silence that happened. 'This is where she would have stood to make it.'

We shivered, shaking our arms and legs about like children to get rid of the queer dream feeling cast onto the day.

A fragile blessing? Might we find a stable form of friendship in this year ahead, after everything? What I wrote in my diary once home, still afflicted by my fatal capacity to wait, and hope.

But we were never together again.

§

It was just a few days after Trekkie's view and I was alone on the side of Firle Beacon, Caburn's neighbour, among the jackdaws and rooks that had been the only things to hold my attention in the winter months without the wild woman's book. Up there, in the loose and unruly company of those birds, I could look back at the town where I'd made myself too known, and pinch it between my thumb and finger. Shrink it in significance. The hillside as a place of safe remove, where I could be without role or reputation. Quiet, calm.

Now though, my heart was pounding. Adrenaline, anger, resolve.

Minutes earlier, I'd been in the village church down below.

So many years after the near-death, it was only now that I'd begun to read books on faith and consider whether my dream life – with its insistent vision of grace offered and refused across a threshold – had been pointing me in the right direction all along.

Of all the unlocked churches in the surrounding area, only that one was free of the smells and shadows which always had me turn away, hackles raised, at their entrance. (Used to the Methodist chapels of my childhood – bread plain, barn simple – the buildings of this region were too dark, too rich for my instincts.) And even here, in this airiest one, the idea of ever attending a Sunday service remained both remote and oppressive, but I'd started to call in on weekdays before or after my time among the birds on the Beacon.

Much as I'd been as a child when asking Mother to take me to my great-aunts and elderly neighbours, only to have exhausted my interest within moments: how I was there usually. I'd play a few chords on the guitar left out in the children's corner, or run my fingers along the kneeling cushions stitched with otters, hares and herons, then go.

But on this day, I'd come to sit on the vestry floor and think, looking up at the blue and gold light of its bright John Piper window. *Homage to William Blake's Book of Job.* Broken sun, crescent moon. Sheep lying asleep underneath, with only one that has its eyes open, looking out.

Job 28:12. *But where shall wisdom be found? and where* is *the place of understanding?*

The Bible in my hand was pocket-sized with a cracked spine and its coloured illustrations coming loose. Among the things I'd carried away from Granny Shadrick's house, I took it for the only scraps of her handwriting I could find before leaving there forever: her mother's month and year of death, recorded in blue ink on the inside cover.

But where shall wisdom be found? and where is *the place of understanding?*

There I sat, feeling stupid to be preoccupied by such unworldly things when outside I could hear a tractor reversing, and a delivery lorry unloading by the brewing company, and the blacksmith at her work. Everybody busy with the business of living.

Effort hadn't cured me. Love hadn't. The peace and clear purpose I had been searching for, and was trying now simply to live without. Might I find it here, after everything?

Faith and farming. Sermons, singing and the tending of sheep. What had held my granny and the women of her line safe for generations. With all my freedoms, I envied her and them that hedge- and hymn-bound living. The rhythm of those days.

Perhaps I could just pretend at it, loving now this one church and village as I did. Give up my resistance to the idea of a God the Father, if only to become part of a tradition which, for all its misuses, had these beautiful buildings for offering aid and refuge?

I opened the Bible again. Hoping – all those years after the haemorrhage and my glimpse of the inhabited light – for a sign, a wonder.

Leviticus 12:1–8. All about birth, and bleeding and impurity: how unclean a woman is after delivering a son, and how much longer soiled by bearing a daughter. The *sin offering* and atonement needed so she can return to the tabernacle, and before which *she shall touch no hallowed thing*.

Fear felt as presence, near and threatening. Like a rabbit

caught out in the open, I looked up at the vaulted ceiling as if a bird might be coming, clawed, towards me.

But remembered then my own blood, how wet and heavy the bed sheet when it hit the hospital floor. And Granny not being allowed to hold her stillborn child. The delicious smell of my daughter when delivered. There was no sin in any of this. Nothing to atone for.

My place is outside.

Words from my repeating dream shouted out loud as my legs took me *away away* in a fury of exclusion. Forcing me up the steep side of the Beacon, lungs hurting, while cursing men, bloody men, and their institutions.

Halfway up, out of breath, I turned towards the valley and gave the universe another chance to answer. Aware of how mad I was in that moment, a middle-aged woman, shouting at the sky.

'HERE I AM, GOD.'

Clouds shifted. Light poured through.

Caburn, illuminated.

I laughed. At myself. Unholy bloody fool. Whatever there was – or was not – beyond this, it would never relieve me of the need to make choices. Each day. In my family, our town, this landscape.

My phone made a sound then in my pocket, and I read the text.

Him.

Evasion. Postponement. Humour falling wide of its mark.

I didn't lose my temper. It was more deadly than that. My wish for his company would always be this way: the pair of red shoes in fable that have the girl who wears them dance herself to destruction. I just kept coming to his call, didn't I?

Beyond this point, there is no honour in it.

What Nye had said before Christmas, noticing a sadness on my face before I could hide or disguise it. *There was some, Tan, in what you asked for and attempted after Switzerland – even if*

I'm the only person in the world who would see it so. But now? There's not.

Beyond this point, then: there was no honour in it.

And because I would always forgive this man anything, waiting for his every return, it was up to me to become it, instead. *Unforgiveable.* So it must be done in a manner that left us no way back, even if I went to his door repentant, pleading, in another week or month or season.

I had to cut him off – there and then – to save myself and the new year just begun, even if it would feel like an amputation.

That is how it felt – irreparable, and brutal, like axe blows aimed at him and me both – to send a message back which did what I had never done to a person before, and never will again. Taking every true and sad and awful regret he'd ever confided to me about his life and using them against him. Knowing from my near-death how distressing that would be.

A flaying that was deep and neat and deliberate: what I'd thought seeing the vandalised tree years ago, I did now to that man I still cared for, after everything. How cruel I was, how ugly. Inflicting pain to save my own soul.

As his reply, a single word. After all the thousands we'd shared, it was the last he'd ever send me.

Romance of Maintenance

AFTER THAT MESSAGE, sent with surgical intent from the hillside, I went back to my home and stayed there. The whole first month of that new year.

I enjoyed, in those weeks, and unexpectedly, a post-operative calm: that clean and tender feeling brought back from hospital when emptied of a thing that had to go. I'd cry still with want for him, but never again like before, when there was always a little hope. Hard to understand though he'd been, this in him I did know: he would never forgive me the words I'd written.

And so it was over, at last.

Gone, too, and more importantly, was the string in me that had been there all my life, since earliest girlhood: that longing for a man who might save me, if I stayed always small in one small place where I could be found. This deep-rooted and unreasonable hunger that even a long and loving marriage to a man my own age could not meet; that had made of me a goat tethered to a stake of my own making, so that I'd rather eat bare the grass in a near circle around me than risk going free and unfound in the world.

Now, where it had been, it was not. And so the self which had been tied to it – that was gone too.

Unlike the first painful breaths I had to perform for an audience of doctors and nurses at the start of my second life, there was no one there to witness the beginning of this, my third. It was quiet and invisible, all internal feeling. No one, not even Nye yet, could tell the difference there was in me, and this is why I stayed inside. Biding my time. Taking stock. Making sure.

§

Once Nye and the children were gone to work and school each day, I began to examine all the artefacts and relics of our shared life. Methodically, starting with the basement and its sedimentary layers of our children's cast-off younger selves. Plastic tub of Playmobil figures. Picture books without which they once upon a time would never go to sleep. Photos back from when we bothered to print them – gone damp and curled at the edges. End-of-term reports and the overfull folders from the nursery years, showing grubby-faced babies in kitchens and sandpits. Books about self-sufficiency and do-it-yourself given by Nye and me, each to each, when our handwriting was as smooth and round as our faces. And this one in particular: *How Buildings Learn: What happens after they're built.* Where we'd found the notion of a romance of maintenance, and taken it for ourselves. Precious to me all over again now, what Nye had written inside it twenty years before, given all we'd just been through:

As buildings learn, so do lovers. Strange to think of us in the years ahead, accumulating photos of our skin, our structure and sites – watching how we will have changed. One thing will always stay the same: the stuff of us, and our love. Sometimes rearranged, but forever there, on deep foundations.

How far back we went together could be seen best in his grandfather's trunk, which lived now at the foot of the marriage bed.

Almost empty when Nye and I met and began to make love in his student room, now it was stuffed full to bursting, so that if we ever looked into it, someone had to sit on top afterwards to squeeze shut the metal latches.

I opened it now and took out every last thing, covering the floor around me. Memory game. *Look, look, at what you've made together.*

My tawny-coloured dress of field and flowers I wore on our first long walk across the Downs, before I lay in the woods, waiting for Nye to start undoing the buttons.

His original brown trousers.

Our first love letters.

Wedding dress, with my grandfather's footprints still on it. Nye's shirt and tie from that day.

The plastic name shackles I'd cut free from my son, then me. His umbilicus stump, his sister's. Their first pyjamas, their favourite T-shirts from every summer.

Cards given to Granny by Grandad Shadrick during their seven-year courtship.

Nothing whatsoever of any monetary worth.

But it restored to me now a sense of who I was. Who I belonged to and what I meant to them. What they meant to me, too.

§

After everything we owned had been touched by me and tidied in this way, after that, I looked at my messages.

How many had come in from friends and strangers in the months when I was hiding up on the hillside with heartbreak and shame, using the wild woman's book and its aftermath as excuse for my rudeness.

But now that same undertaking – *Wild Woman Swimming* – became my way back to the world. There were residencies I was encouraged to apply for on the strength of it. I'd been sent reminders of the last few readings I had to give, as well as a deadline for submitting the book to a major nature-writing prize.

Readers got in touch asking, shyly, politely, if I'd be willing to meet them, even just once. The many people who'd helped me make it – was I free to walk with them, now the project was done and winter easing?

I filled in every last form. Entered the book for the prize. Applied to be the writer-in-residence at a midsummer literary festival and confirmed I was available still to be in Virginia Woolf's garden the same week. Accepted an invitation from two retired hospice doctors to stay on their small private island in Canada, and another from a woman skilled in the ways of plants and animals who lived in the French Alps. Planned a haiku-writing day for schoolchildren in a beautiful bird hide at a nature reserve where I was already its visiting writer.

And said *yes, please, thank you for asking me* to every single miraculous person, known to me or not, who wanted my company.

From the early years of mothering, I knew how much time it would take, and how shy I would feel, learning these new people who wanted to meet me. And how humbling it would be to return to friends from before who'd find me now so fragile and changed. But I was glad of the chance to begin again, and even looked forward to the discomfort. It would demand effort of the best kind: the sort that builds into things honest and lasting, which can be shared. And I would never again let the life around me – home, family, friendships – fall into disrepair through a mistaken attachment to a wrong idea.

Stay This Moment

A WOMAN WITHOUT FEET. How I thought of myself at midsummer, still only half a year free from a lifetime chasing after scraps of love.

And what a wonderful occupation for a woman not able to walk: to be holding court for the day in Monk's House, last home of Virginia Woolf.

Earlier, I'd sat at her desk and been photographed. Aware – even while my face ached with pleasure – of how unlikely the scenario: me from a class that would have made me her servant – the village girl who came in daily to empty the ashes, light the stove, sweep the floors. Having to dip my knee when spoken to, as my Granny Nell had to bob and curtsey for the squire who employed her as cook.

Instead, visitors had begun to gather around my travelling table just outside her studio, waiting for me, the living writer, to speak. I opened her diaries and began to read, in an accent so different to hers:

> If one does not lie back and sum up and say to the moment, this very moment, stay you are so fair, what will be one's gain, dying? No: stay this moment. No one ever says that enough. Always hurry. I am now going in, to see Leonard and say stay this moment.

After this, I invited my audience to take a board, pencil and some paper. To savour, as she did, the sensation of being there, in that garden full of flowers with its view across the Downs. To go home having taken part in something, it being the national day of celebration for writing come around again. *Stay this moment.*

At first, no one stepped forward, so I simply smiled at my hands and waited without worry for their hesitation to give way, as I knew it would.

Unlike Woolf, a life of letters was nothing I was born to, and yet how entirely at home I felt in those grounds, that exercise.

A long-married Dutch couple went to sit side by side where Leonard and Virginia played bowls during wartime (having to throw themselves to the ground sometimes when fighter planes came too low or crashed nearby). This husband and wife were giggling like children and hiding their paper from one another because I'd said I would post his to her *the next day* – it might even arrive back in Europe before them – but would make *him* wait a long, long time for *hers*.

Beside me a man sat chewing his pencil while thinking how to thank his sister for taking on the main care of their elderly parents so he was free always to travel and work.

Only two years before, I'd been beside the pool having set many of its sunbathers to this same task. And the note I wrote there at early evening, just as the weather broke: I lived in the aftermath of that now, its wreckage; what took flight for such a short while having left pieces of me all over the local landscape. My feet on Firle Beacon; a bit of green headscarf caught on gorse by a clifftop bench with a view to the Seven Sisters; my shadow held fast by another on a concrete path, reached across railway tracks, that leads through a derelict village to the sea; in a work-shop on the far edge of the Downs, hairpins of mine I could never now retrieve.

What had I learned from all this? Was I wise yet after so much wasted time, and so many errors? What was my credo? Did I have one?

To make fun from nothing, and meaning from the simplest of materials. To share whatever is learned. To move, with suppleness, between the silly and the serious: not to get stuck in a pose of one or the other.

What I wrote, in line with Mount Caburn, before lying back in one of the striped deckchairs put out for visitors, eyes closed, simply enjoying the hum of people at work.

Wondering then if Woolf's last words to Leonard might be made over in a happier way as gift to Nye in a week that was also the twenty-fifth anniversary of our love at first sight. (Our plan was simply to eat chips on the nearby bridge at Southease, feet swinging over the river Ouse – where her body had been found, but in too beautiful a view to avoid ever after as morbid.)

The greatest possible happiness . . . You have been entirely patient and incredibly good.

Yes. True of her husband, and true of mine too.

Although not of me.

You're a Catherine wheel, and I'm the fucking nail. Write that down! What Nye had said in an unguarded moment while I packed in a whirl for my week of public events at home and away, giddy with news that the wild woman's book had made it onto the longlist for the nature-writing prize. She – *and me as her editor!* – sitting alongside authors who were household names.

I stopped and turned to him.

A second of silence – *how unfailingly kind we'd been in the seasons since my other love and its ending* – but then laughter – *helpless, excessive, unstoppable* – so that we rolled around on the

floor together, gasping with it. The return of humour, and rudeness, and the sort of tumbling, jumpers-rucked lovemaking we'd
enjoyed at our start. A rough celebration, the work of moments.
How we knew we'd made it through.

Wing Brushes Cheek

A MOTHER AND DAUGHTER walk alone together, barefoot, on a chalk path that runs behind their favourite village, for the simple pleasure of walking up it and then back, sandals in hand, having to look, *really look*, at the stones and choose a way through them.

The mother bonded with her first child through song, and it is still what they use in rare moments when he's home and without his headphones. He grabs hold of her at those times, and they dance like bears in the kitchen, his head already a head above hers. They are clumsy, all paws. Her writing hand has become too strong, he tells her. She clumps him with it when she means to be gentle. As a pair, they are silly like this. Never sad.

Daughter lives in a different dimension: absorbed in colour, form, texture, line. Everything going in at the eye, and out through the hand that draws, so that she prefers to spend time together quietly, side by side. Or sitting, back turned, in the bath where she allows her long hair to be conditioned and combed, while considering ways to render water, or bubbles, in pencil, on a flat surface.

She has stopped now, this girl walking ahead, the better to speak and be heard (a habit of her deliberate nature). And what she says is a single word.

It goes up, like a pheasant or jay flushed from cover.

A name. Into the air; harsh and bright, alarming. *His name.*

The mother stands, hand on throat.

We knew, you know, says the girl.

They look deeply into this.

I'm so ashamed. What the mother begins to say, but daughter steps forward and her hand is a wing brushing cheek. Grace. Pure and unmerited.

You were in the basement, that Christmas. Asking someone not to abandon you. We thought at first it was your father.

What a failure of mothering, the mother says, *to have caused you that worry.*

We weren't. Not for us. We knew you wouldn't go where we couldn't find you.

What to say?

The truth.

Like the lines her girl can place on a page, light yet sure, so that something astonishing unfolds upon it; how the mother attempts now to lay out her life between them.

Saying, *yes*, she'd been sad, but for a long time, and before all that, however often she was happy. *Which was often.* It was an old, old problem that no amount of love freely given ever solved. It was just something stuck in her from when she was much smaller than the daughter was now. But it was gone at last, and that had been the ugly way it worked itself out. She'd had to appeal to that man – to his pity – as she'd never allowed herself, as a girl, with her father. She'd had to learn, as a woman, that it *wouldn't have worked*, to ask or to beg, the first time, either. Did she understand?

Yes, I think we knew that too, the daughter says.

Their path has been walked up, and back.

They sit in the white dust to buckle their sandals. Deciding to buy after this flowers from a house in the village, as is their other shared pleasure.

The shapes they leave on the chalk are two white birds, the ghosts of them, and will do, the mother thinks, as epitaph for the love which lies behind her.

A Golden String

WE WERE BACK IN THE CHAPEL of the sculptor and his wife, when summer was ended and my engagements over. Behind me, already and so soon: that vintage season in Virginia Woolf's garden and the other places I'd been invited to visit as maker of the wild woman's book.

I didn't know how to feel about life after that week: my happiness was on a wavelength that I, always striving, hadn't discovered on the dial before – it was *blank* (like my calendar). An absence of strain, obligation, ambition. A quietude. And so that I could let it expand into the space available, instead of simply filling it with a binge of online reading, I went down to the studio below our guest quarters: not the sculptor's, but his wife's.

Although it had been him I met first, and in a way that altered the course of my life, it was her art now, not his, that always called forth my strongest feelings.

Alone among her work, as I was allowed to be, I went like a cat through a garden, investigating every texture and smell – the wet paint left mixed in pots under cling film, the coloured dust that had crumbled off in the pastel boxes. Tasted, even, a few small bits of chalk and charcoal.

Went then to another of her rooms, and there they were, as I remembered them.

Sleepers and Dreamers.

Figure after figure, large ones and small, done in ochres and umbers, siennas burnt and raw, cadmium yellows, Indian reds.

I loved listening to her talk about these colours: how she spoke of them as *aspects of earth and air* that had to be *introduced to the room and each other* every time she began to paint.

I lay down then, to be likewise attentive to the figures around me. Draped forms, all of them, veiled and sensual. Cocooned, in chrysalis. Enfolded in rest and acceptance. Entire unto themselves. Neither waiting nor hoping. Not enticing, or turning away. Undisturbed and simply there, in their element.

Oh. This is how it had been for me once, so long ago.

Before the school years and the awful arguments that began with Mother's mistaken second marriage, there had been that brief prelapsarian time when I could be with Granny. Free in those few seasons to touch all my hands desired: cotton reels, beads, neck scarves in colours like the ones now on the walls around me.

Relieved, while there, of the need to contain my needs.

Back home, my hunger for touch had only ever been a threat and danger to the fragile peace that depended, for Mother, on everything remaining forever in its right place. Whereas it was my natural tendency – I remembered now, among my friend's figures – to be wordless and absorbed in the pursuit of form and light and colour, as artists and sculptors are, as my daughter was. Those woollen threads I wove so intently through my grandmother's rooms to keep company with the sun as it moved: my first work of art. But I turned away from that into words on paper. The black and the white. That neater, cleaner way to show love for the world and what's in it.

I give you the end of a golden string; only wind it into a ball. Blake, who I had, at last and so late, begun to read. And here was mine, waiting for the time when I might stop driving myself onwards, outwards. The memory of those webs of coloured wool leading me back to a way I could be at peace from now on.

Because it would be enough, *more than enough*, to be a person occupied for the rest of my life by what might look to others only an idiotically simple gathering in of small and obscure moments: the collecting of stories from ordinary people like me.

Back upstairs again, I sat, hands on lap, like a patient in a waiting room, listening to the rain, my heart, and the voices of others I'd met in that last good year.

Write a book. You must. What more and more people had been saying to me, so that I held up my empty palms each time saying, *I don't know how to start.*

Nor did I still. But it seemed obvious then, on that last afternoon of summer, that I could at least share the good I'd been given by the sculptor. What he had told me, that made me feel able to try what none of my family ever had: *to make things from nothing, out of my own particular concerns*; I could pass this on so others might get use from it too.

Hours it took, with the unsteady signal in the guest cottage, to send out and away just some of the much that I'd learned from him:

THE SCULPTOR'S ADVICE FOR ART AND LIFE

Always give your ideas 'molecules', quickly, before they fade: just a title is enough, or a sketch, or a few notes on scrap paper, sellotaped up and kept in view. In this way, a thing beyond your time, resources, or abilities now, is far more likely to happen in future.

Be professional and serious in your work, however late and tentative your endeavours.

Measure success not by the number of people who respond to what you make but be motivated instead by that one

*necessary person you might meet, whenever you risk putting
a well-intentioned work into the world.*

*Be moved, also, by the possibility of becoming that person to
others.*

*Tell a true, ongoing story of your life as well as your art.
Even if you receive no reward or notice for what you do, you
still gain meaning from this, and purpose.*

*Understand how much time it takes for a work, or a path,
or a life to take shape.*

Be alert to the teachings of chance.

I published it as a long online thread and turned off my
phone. Last night of our holidays, and an early start in the
morning for home. Work then for Nye, school for the children.
No plans at all for me, who had clung to them for dear life my
first forty years.

*Your writing earlier was exceptional. I can't wait to receive
some form of something. Might it be coming soon?*

What I saw when I logged on the next day at five in the
morning before our car drove away from the chapel – sent by an
agent who'd been intrigued by me at my outside writing table
in one of the gardens I'd performed in over summer. (We'd had
lunch in London soon afterwards, but I had no proposal to offer
and came away believing it only a delicious glimpse of a world
I might have belonged to if I'd been braver and brighter, years
ago, after graduation.)

'Are you going to write a book of your own next, Mum?' Our
son, from the back seat, after hearing me read Nye the message.

I smiled in the dark.

'Oh, lovey. I've had a good run these last few years, but I'm out of ideas now, and energy. Time, I think, to see if anyone will give me a desk job again, if I can scrub up after so long outside, barefoot, wearing aprons.'

Through the window, only just visible, mountains and valleys endlessly repeating. How strange to imagine clocking in and out of a single building after all my wild, free seasons. To put myself back into harness. I tried not to mind, but I did.

'You started a story once, Mum. I liked the title.' Son again, awake still even though he was insensate usually on those early morning starts. 'THE CURE FOR SLEEP. That was the one. Try it when we're home.'

LAST RITES

Bringest thou life or death?
Or haply cut me short for good?
Or leave me here as now?

Waking in the Dark

UP BEFORE DAWN, off-grid and alone in a shepherd's hut, I reach for my matches.

The candle I light sits in a blue enamel holder that was my mother's when a girl. What she carried upstairs to bed, I take now for courage to wherever I go in my late-made writing life. Since my solitary weeks in the Swiss treehouse, I have learned that nights are always the price of my days. And I've accepted that I may always be scared of the dark, but I don't any more let it stop me from going away. Instead, whenever my nerve fails after dusk or before sunrise in a new and remote place, I light a candle and watch its flame waver and settle until I am steadfast too.

I look now at the hand holding the match and I circle it this way, that. *Still there, and working.* In the night it was taken off clean at the wrist, so that I carried it about in my left one, help-less. This repeating motif through my whole childhood made urgent, and appalling, through dream code: how my father as a young man, disinherited from the family farm, was told *he had his hands* and could be a mechanic; how I, clever, in the next generation was taught by Mother and my teachers that *I wouldn't need mine.*

Knowing then that *here it was*, the great decisive moment of my life. Concluding, in sleep, that writing – the expression of belief – is, after all, a manual labour no less than the care of farm animals and small children. And need not be the severance from family and class I always feared. Or if it is, then I'm ready now to bear those losses.

§

Who am I then, and where, this woman awake in her only and third life who is writing a book at last, after reading so many for so long?

Here, in this wooden room on wheels, it the end of January in a year when my small country begins its retreat from Europe. In the silence I feel the hut and my tiny island drift away from the protections and constraints of being joined with those other countries.

How shrunken life has begun to feel: resources and freedoms being daily stripped away. It is so easy to feel inert and without purpose. What use any one small soul?

But then a phrase from my time as a hospice scribe returns to me: *It's not much, but neither is it nothing.* And so I will try and write a book of my own, inch by inch, that might reach beyond my narrow self and add to the ration of courage that stories are for us all. To share this learning I have, which was only accidental at first, back when I painted the railings: that more of us might find more and many little ways to step out from our circles of safe belonging, to show and share what we know, and surprise interest from others who encounter us. To be people who simply sit on park benches, open and noticing, so that a lonely person might feel able to risk a smile, then take a seat and speak. To spend even a few of our spare hours in this way, being calling cards and quiet invitations.

And for me, fatherless, who circled so long his absence, waiting for a man who might replace him? How can I better use my years remaining?

I want, I think, to become a landmark, myself, so that anyone reading this in my lifetime might travel here to find me aproned and headscarved, going along the chalk paths, over ridges, to the river. I want people to call my name and start a conversation. This will do for my work, however else I may have to earn my money.

And it's not, after all, a vocation handed me by divine revelation as I used to yearn for, nor an inherited role as Granny enjoyed on her farm. Neither does it come with any qualification, as the achievements of my first life yielded. It's simply a way of using better what is best in me: my ability to listen and remember – a skill for helping others into voice and possibility.

As with the circle at the centre of those blankets I make at decisive times, so then I begin this story that might one day be held or heard by people I won't even know. A tale that will turn around this chapter, accruing stories, until what I have in my hand is book-length and book-shaped.

(And what a thing a book is! How far it can travel, like a seed that carries on a wing or the wind to germinate in another time and place.)

Like a seed myself, I'm in a field beside the church at the foot of Firle Beacon, settled into one of the deeply female folds that lie between the ridges that are all along these Sussex Downs, my adopted home this last quarter-century.

When I arrived here as a student so many years ago, I wanted – like Woolf – to get free of a father's shadow and write myself into a landscape through works that would survive me.

Few things finer. What I thought then, as a girl who grew up on farmland with no prospect of owning it.

What I think still.

In My Beginning Is My End

'DO YOU LOVE ME?'

The terrible question. Asked only ever *in extremis* and when everything depends on it.

What my mother is asking me now, in the early autumn of a plague year.

Almost eighty and newly alone in the last of the bleak, outlying houses she has chosen during her forty-year marriage to release a little equity each time, she is in a terminal state: divorcing for the start of her ninth decade, with crippled feet and small savings that are about to be halved. The house, too, must be sold and the proceeds likewise divided.

This is our endgame. She knows it, I know it.

It is late in the evening on the last day of a wild week together – the only visit I've been able to make to her in six months of infection risk and travel restrictions.

There is a plastic bag on the kitchen table between us, punctured by a murder of knives and forks, all thrown together too quickly, and lethal now for being so – cause of this night's bitter fight: what cutlery to keep. And yet this is why I'm here: to help her do what she cannot: fetch and carry, choose and sort. Because although the surfaces in her home are as immaculate as those in the houses of my childhood – polished daily free of dust and fingerprints – the cupboards and drawers have always held another story.

§

Our first day had gone well. We went together to a big town and I did what she'd never let me do before: buy her some new clothes. *Whatever you want, Mum, I'll put it on a card.* And it felt good, once she'd agreed, to see her made so happy from choosing just a few inexpensive things.

But then, on return, when I opened a wardrobe to put her new things away and begin then on what I was really there to do, that is where our trouble started.

It would all just have to come out onto the floor, I said. Every wardrobe was packed too tight with hangers for me to sort the pieces on their rails. *Was she going to be OK about that?*

And it was this – my bringing to light big armfuls of clean and mostly unworn outfits, many of them still tagged – that triggered her panic, and then the anger which followed on from it always.

Put it back. Put it back. Or put it all this minute instantly into bin bags for the dump.

She wouldn't leave me alone to do it, but neither could she bear to see it done. And this was the plight which had paralysed her life: unable to bear the brief disorder caused by tidying out a cupboard, her cupboards were therefore full of things which oppressed her. Such cabin pressure it created in those airless rooms with their windows kept shut against dust from the road, just as we'd once sealed ourselves into the bungalow's bedroom each night to keep safe from intruders.

Had she had any plan of her own for all this? What I asked next, as I knelt between the bales of clothing, feeling the weight of our past in the present.

If you must know, I wanted to die here and leave it all for you to deal with once I was buried in the ground.

Said to me in a mutinous tone, arms folded.

That is how the days went on.

And all the time, she telling me how awful it had always been, the marriage that was ending, until on that last night I'd said I didn't think I could do it any more. Be in her life. I wouldn't leave in the morning, then keep her waiting for a decision, but would make it tonight. And whatever I decided, I would always support her in practical ways, from a distance. But this? Listening to endless outpourings of misery, when I myself had barely survived it, living with them? *No.*

What on earth did I mean? She said.

Pillar of salt.

What I wanted her to become from the fury of my look. I wished for her, yes, to be struck down in retribution for all of it.

And it felt biblical like that – a last judgement and our day of reckoning – when I answered her back.

With a deadly gin-trap force, I said that if everything she'd said about how it had been for her was true – *then it was also true that it happened to me too.*

Because I had been there, with them. Hearing, seeing. There had been a child in those rooms of their desolate houses. A child who felt obliterating fear in proximity to their anger, but had no means of escaping it, for years. There had been a child there. *It was me.*

§

'Do you love me?'

And that is how we arrived, in the last hours of my week's visit, at this terminal question – her panic at my emptying of the cutlery drawers having provoked us to this sudden end of everything, so that we are sitting stunned now, side by side, at the table.

What to say?

I want to say that I *told her* – at the start of the year, when I'd been given a miraculous book deal for what was then just a title and a few thousand words – I told her then, *I would not be stopped*. That unless my husband, or my children or I somehow fell seriously ill or died, that I would allow nothing to come between me and what I had waited so long to attempt. *I would not be stopped*. But lo and behold! This very year it was happening finally, the dissolution of their awful yet enduring marriage. And just as I was least free or willing to help, so that I wonder now if something other than their months-long misery of having to stay at home and alone together has brought her and my step-father to this late but abrupt parting.

I want to ask – *queasy possibility* – if this book has made it happen? Does she want to *rewrite* her role in it?

I want to say that since this crisis began, my dreams are all of a vast and implacable darkness. No visual element, only an oceanic sense of a great ship going down and me in the nearby water, and not even as a lifeboat but only a bundle of sticks and rope. My self become a structure not fit to save anyone.

There is so much I want to say. I say nothing.

'Tell me the truth now. Am I just a problem for you?'

What to say?

I put a hand around my throat, restraining myself.

How easy it would be to bring the house down on our heads. For my sharp tongue to let fly words like knives, as I did on the hill at Firle Beacon, when cutting free from that other painful presence in my life.

But also: how tempting to voice a kind lie on this decisive night that might avoid more pain now, while preventing any hope of change hereafter.

I breathe.

In. Out. Deciding.

'I did love you. A long time ago. So very much. And could again perhaps once this is all done and we are come through it.'

In this moment I am almost fifty and not yet ten. I bow my neck, afraid, and wait with both my selves for her tears, her rage.

Instead she is dry-eyed and silent. Suddenly calm, as I can't ever remember her.

'I don't know you, really, do I?' What she says next, with an almost regal look. A new space opens up between us, she in her seat, me in mine.

What is happening here?

Are we, finally, about to become two sovereign women in negotiation? Using the same rules of engagement for the first time, and discovering new moves on the board? If we are, then I will risk a bold one.

'No. You don't know me, I think, even though I've never kept any secrets from you. There was always too much noise between you and him, and what is most real in me runs deep, and is quiet. But I will show you, if you want. How I think. What I have thought about you.'

And this is how I find myself reading from a book still not finished, which she fears.

I tell her about us in bed together on the edge of those unheeding fields. About her endeavours before me, and her beauty. How wonderful she was with the only man she ever loved, the one she sacrificed in error. The day when she talked like a child, so that my own childhood ended.

I wait then for the sky to fall – this thing my first life was always protecting against. Rules and routines: my scaffold, my roof beams.

'How could you have seen all that, and understood? That is exactly how I was with him. So much fun and kindness.'

She goes out and comes back in, carrying something. She places it on the table. It is a photo of her and him, that man she loved and let go, hidden away all these years so I'd forgotten, really, what he looked like.

I laugh. Dear God.

He looks *so very like* the man who surprised such late and devastating love in me.

How funny, how awful it all is.

I tell her what a marvellous, humbling joke life has just played on me. I say we should gather up, right now, whatever other few artefacts she has from him and make of them – now she is alone here – a little collection, in one place. Where she can see them every day and remember what had once been good.

Well. That dictionary over there that's falling apart now, he bought it for her, loving crosswords as much as she did. She has two of his brown handkerchiefs at the back of a drawer upstairs. And – she goes away and comes back again – *this.*

I am dumbfounded.

It is an exquisite oriental teapot with a delicate wicker handle and fine brown patterning all around it. It is so very beautiful and like nothing else in the whole overstuffed and unhappy house. An entire other life that might have been is held there.

I have never seen it before. It has survived everything.

We place it in the middle of a newly emptied bookshelf, across from where she sits in daytime to read her papers, and then just stand there, side by side, looking at it.

'Oh why didn't you marry him and move away? Just dragging me with you?' What I ask before I can stop myself. How cruel of me, though I didn't mean to be. *Oh the pity of it.* It is the most terrible thing that lies between her and me: that I, at six, told her to marry him and leave me behind.

'I was scared to go away and live in a city, is the truth of it. And didn't think I could ask him to turn down the job he was offered. Then, once I'd married the wrong man and all that began happening so fast, he came to the bungalow and said I should just bloody leave and he would stand beside me and look everyone in the face, if I would.'

'You had another chance? Oh why, why, didn't you go? For both our sakes?'

'Well here's the other truth of it: I'd been divorced once already and I knew what it was like to be talked about, even when it was no fault of my own. And I just couldn't bear the idea of people doing it again.'

Forty years.

I feel for her hand and hold it, tight. Because only now am I a woman who can understand what that really means, having myself so recently been stricken to the point of deathly self-neglect from losing the good opinion of a dear friend.

But, still. All that time.

And they talked about us anyway.

Back at the kitchen table, she reaches for my hand next.

Says, little girl in an old body of a sudden – like Granny when she asked for my help to die – that it's all right, I can walk away now. She accepts, tonight, the harm she has done me. That it is too late for her. I should go and not come back.

I could. There is no debt, and I feel no guilt. And no part of me, on this night, wants it – to be giving care in my own home or a nearby flat to a long-distant mother precisely as I have just come clear of illness, and young children, and heartbreak. What was good in her life so long ago, I have honoured now in writing. It is enough.

So what then is bringing calm to my hands that have been shaking? Not an epiphany, sudden as a shaft of light, but rather a slow clearing of my sight so I can see how my mother's hands look now like *her* mother's – not hard and relentless, as I knew them in the years of her wiping my face and brushing my hair against its grain but soft now and arthritic at the fingertips, like the joints in her feet that once did long shop hours in the highest of heels while she earned just enough to feed us both.

And then I am thinking of Nye sitting opposite me in the big picture window in Switzerland asking not *when* and *where* and *how could you* but: *What are you trying to do? What do you need to find peace?*

I think of my young daughter on the chalk path, and the

elegant way she sent my other love's name into that summer sky. Showing me, with such lightness of touch, that she knew about him. Releasing me in this way from any burden of blame or shame.

I decide I can do it.

Go home and prepare a place for her there, my mother, should she want or need it, once the long legal proceedings are completed.

Not because I'm a daughter, and her only child.

Nor for any scales in a hereafter that might weigh our lives, with me balancing mine by doing for this woman what I could not for my grandmother.

Nor from fear of what others will think if I walk away.

I will do it because we are here, now, together, and alone, after everything. Fully awake, both of us, and for the first time, to who we really are.

And because I am aware, now at this table in a dark kitchen by a fast road, of the forces that have borne down on each of us, differently, and without cease, from the moments of our birth, on her no less than me, so that it is simply a miracle if any of us find our way back through the tangle and crush of it all to our true natures. And rarer still if we can arrive at them together and keep company there.

Mother gets in to bed and I kiss her goodnight. Take myself next to the guest room where I lie awake, without worry. One in the morning. Two.

At three I pack for the drive home to Nye and our children, and go downstairs, alone, to make tea: this simple thing my son has managed in our home for years, which I have never felt able to do in any of my mother's houses. Obeying, on every visit, the old rules of childhood, decades after I'd grown and gone.

With the cup in my hands, I understand that I am come back to where I began, but arrived now at my right size and shape. One that can hold myself and others safe. That after all my experiments in living, there is a marriage in me now of responsibility and hope, and that one does not the other cast asunder, as I always believed.

In this moment, my heart is not hurting and my eyes are not tired. But it will be different tomorrow, and for a long while to come: the promise I've just made sets me on another hard road and slow, with no certain destination.

And yet it's enough tonight to feel sure only of this: that when I go from my mother's house next time, she will be with me. Travelling into a new life for her last decade.

This ending I could never have foreseen.

I wash my cup in the sink and leave the drops of water.

ACKNOWLEDGEMENTS

Personal Acknowledgements

FROM THE TIME BEFORE, I THANK: my mother, for our years alone together, and for the courage she is showing now in her own late-woken life. Mrs Cornish and Dr Alistair Davies: first fine teacher, and last.

FROM THE TIME SINCE: Emma Chaplin, for holding my hand. Molly Booth, who smiled back, and with whom I learned how to mother. Wise counsellors Richard Price and Matt Ingrams, who both – one at each end of a decade – told me to tell stories. Jeremy Page, Alexandra Loske and Steve Thorp: first publishers to believe in my words. Claire and David Nash for their love and humour, and showing me how to balance life and art. Steve Creffield, for his dream of me as a wounded healer, and photographing me in the attempt so many years later. Mathew Clayton, who told me how to make a book. Vera Michalski-Hoffmann, for my weeks in another country: that time among the staff, fellow residents and books at Fondation Jan Michalski was transformative. Writers Philippe Rahmy (who died just days after my return from Switzerland) and Lynne Roper, wild woman swimming: the two gone ones – even brief time in their company altered me for good. Jenny and Mike Roper for trusting me with their daughter's work. Louisa Archer, Jenny Arran, John Bennett, Louisa Thomsen Brits, Toby Chown, Kerri ní Dochartaigh, Lulah Ellender, Neil Gower, Jo Sweeting and Carole Villiers – the artists and writers who walk and talk magic rings round me. Adam Nicolson, for telling me – as if it were the most obvious and achievable thing – that I must write a book of my own once I'd finished with *Wild Woman Swimming*. Robert Caskie, miraculous agent met in strange circumstances a few weeks later, who next dared me to try, so that I did. Peter Owen Jones, for giving me a grace-filled space in which to make the attempt. Paul Braund (strange angel) and Anke Schwittay for being the best possible early readers. All the many skilled and passionate people at Weidenfeld & Nicolson and Orion who worked to have this story reach readers. Most of all: Lettice Franklin, publishing director, for her vision, warmth and trust – I could not have composed this long song of myself and others without her great gift for hearing and seeing the true form for the story.

ALWAYS, ALWAYS, ALWAYS: my son, who made me a mother, and told me to write a book with this title; my daughter, an artist already, who makes something new every day, inspiring me to do so too: boy, girl; hard-won wonder, beautiful surprise. And their father – from our first day till our last – for his passionate commitment to the slow and steadfast work of marriage and writing both: my life's great good fortune that we met.

Permissions Acknowledgements

THE AUTHOR AND THE PUBLISHER would like to thank the Society of Authors as the literary representative of the estate of Virginia Woolf for permission to quote from volume four of her diaries and volume six of her letters.

Lines from Philip Larkin's 'Toads, Revisited' are reprinted by permission of Faber & Faber.

Lines from T.S. Eliot's 'What the Thunder Said' and 'Gerontion' are likewise reprinted by permission of Faber & Faber.

Lines from © Jenny Landreth, 2017, *Swell: A Waterbiography*, Bloomsbury Sport, an imprint of Bloomsbury Publishing plc are also hereby acknowledged, with special thanks to both the author and publisher for their quick and generous permission.

The teller of 'Fox Woman Dreaming' referred to in passing is the acclaimed mythologist and author Dr Martin Shaw.

Quotations from Walt Whitman, Dante and William Blake are taken from online and public domain editions of their work.

About the Author

TANYA SHADRICK is a former hospice scribe who works in public spaces to encourage others to share stories and take creative risks. She has been a visiting writer at many extraordinary places, including England's oldest outdoor pool, Virginia Woolf's garden at Monk's House, and the Jan Michalski Foundation for Writing and Literature in Switzerland. She is editor and publisher of the Wainwright Prize-longlisted *Wild Woman Swimming* (The Selkie Press) and a Fellow of the Royal Society of Arts. This is her first book.